The Myth About
CRIMINAL JUSTICE
DEGREES

How To Get *ANY* Law Enforcement Career Fast

Remember when we were kids and we thought all heroes wore capes and a big "S" on their chest?

Boy, were we wrong.

J I M M Y   M O N K

ISBN: 1492368164
ISBN 13: 9781492368168

Library of Congress Control Number: 2013916392
CreateSpace Independent Publishing Platform
CreateSpace, North Charleston, South Carolina

It only took cartoonist Randy Bish a few minutes to draw this cartoon, but the creation of the idea – an emotional experience for the artist – took much longer.

Bish drew the piece following the shooting death of Pennsylvania State Police Tpr. Paul G. Richey. Bish said he used the words, along with the blank face, to send the message, "These are clothes a hero would wear, like the clothes Superman would wear." The cartoon, which appeared in the January 17, 2010 issue of the *Pittsburgh Tribune-Review* newspaper, is reprinted with Bish's permission. He draws seven sketches a week and credits his ideas for cartoons to junk food and idle hours. (In this author's opinion; his artwork reveals a family man of character, faith and conviction). http://www. politicalcartoons.com/artist/Randy+Bish.html

Trooper Paul Richey was shot and killed when he, and another trooper, responded to a domestic disturbance call in Cranberry Township, Venango County, in Northwestern Pennsylvania. Trooper Richey had served with the Pennsylvania State Police for sixteen years. He is survived by his wife, son, and daughter. Reference: http://www.odmp.org/officer/20232-trooper-paul-garmong-richey#ixzz2F0MQT4TQ

- This information is provided as a tribute to an honorable man and a hero. Please keep his family, and the many more like him, in your thoughts and prayers.

TABLE OF CONTENTS

DEDICATION

This book is dedicated to my entire family, with a strong emphasis on my two sons. I trust in faith that one day they will mature to understand the life lessons I have shared. Until then, I readily acknowledge that both of them assisted me on the journey to become a much better policeman. True fatherhood includes tremendous lessons in pain, humility, and understanding. These young men provided many of those blessings. Life is an experience that teaches patience as you grow through a football field size of measurable mistakes. I remain a student; comforted in the belief that most times I attempted to do everything in my power to show love, support, and the structure needed to guide others. While in contrast, our modern day entitlement-minded society is unknowingly doing very little to support the nucleus of our culture's real success- the family. If law enforcement is your goal, then read this book to achieve some true worldly success. In the process, you should learn a little about money, morality, and faith. Most importantly, you should recognize the price one must pay along the way.

Police work is a higher calling and therefore becomes a higher standard. Self-servers need not apply.

Be a police officer. Work in law enforcement. Make a difference in your community. Wouldn't it be wonderful if you could start earning the salary you deserve right now? If you are interested in a career in law enforcement, this book was written specifically with you in mind. The vital information herein is rarely shared but absolutely necessary to adequately prepare you for a professional law enforcement career. This book was purposely written for college and high school students who are contemplating a career in law enforcement. It is essential for the many military veterans returning to civilian life or, for that matter, any working person who wants to "make a difference." Look inside, read a few pages. I hope you will be inspired to move forward and accomplish your career goals. Learn to be like water flowing over a rock, instead of always swimming upstream.

Definitely a Leader

The key to survival in police work, or any job, is applying your substance, reason for existence, and your meaningful experiences with balance. You are helping me do that here, and I want to thank you. Life-experienced leaders understand people. As a police officer, you are definitely a leader. The world can turn upside down. Take the July 20, 2012, twenty-four year old scumbag loser in Aurora, Colorado who killed Batman movie goers for no reason. I refuse to promote his fame by using his name. We live and function in a society that seemingly demands perfection, as if excellence defines greatness. Yet, it is those who have survived and lived through the emotions of despair, disappointment, and failure who actually know the most. Those who move on are leaders who decide. I classify this as *resilience*. These leaders set a course, execute a goal, or just demand a change. When they drift off course they go back to basics and refocus.

FOREWORD

Any individual contemplating a career in law enforcement would benefit greatly from reading this book. The author speaks from both the practical sense and from the heart. Who better to learn from than someone who has dedicated his life to ensuring the safety and well-being of members of society, as well as fellow officers?

Where you chose to get your "law enforcement education" is clearly an individual choice. This book simply provides practical ways for you to think about how to go about making your choice and possibly save you some hard earned money at the same time. One of the many valuable suggestions that the author gives in this book is to think through the reason you want to enter into a career in law enforcement. It's not glamorous work and the many great things that officers do are often overshadowed by the poor choices of the few; the author speaks to this in a very poignant way.

Helping to clarify your ideas about what a career in law enforcement is about is something the author challenges you to do. Will this be taught in a criminal justice program? Will the program you choose provide you with the real answers about working in law enforcement? The author shares personal experiences, frustrations, and concerns in a candid way throughout this book. One would be wise to listen to his message; he has worked the streets and has witnessed things first hand. You cannot underestimate the value of his experiences.

Having worked within the court system and human services field for many years, I have had endless opportunities to interact with police officers from many jurisdictions. I had the opportunity to work with the author and have found him to be an outstanding individual. Listen to what he is sharing with you and I fully believe it will be a true benefit as you begin to explore a law enforcement career.

Priscilla L. Palmer, M.Ed.

Author Character Endorsement

Steel Valley School District

February 22, 1995

Senior High School

Aldine F. Coleman
Principal

To Whom It May Concern,

This is a letter of reference for James Monk, a former student of mine.
I have known him since his ninth grade year – almost ten years now. What a change I've seen in this young man. From an immature, irresponsible, poorly achieving student to one who was awarded a grant to Point Park College because he had changed dramatically. He was the student that our high school saw great potential in and genuine desire to be successful. Unfortunately for James, and for us, the monies were cut for that program and James was unable to complete four (4) years and no other Steel Valley student has received this award.

Jim is honest, sincere, and conscientious with a great sense of humor. He is loyal to family and friends. God fearing, respectable and concerned about his fellow man and community, I have watched this young man grow from a boy to a man, from a not too serious individual to one who takes life seriously one day at a time; from my student to my friend. What this young man wants to do, his determination and will power drives him towards until he accomplishes his goal. He is determined to be a state policeman; he will be an asset as a policeman and, God willing he will become a state policeman. I have the highest confidence in him and I would recommend him highly.

Very truly yours,

Aldine Coleman

Mrs. Aldine Coleman
Principal

3113 Main Street Munhall, Pennsylvania 15120 (412) 464-3690

"Serving the Educational Needs of Munhall, Homestead and West Homestead"

PART I

The Case Against the

Criminal Justice Degree Program

Chapter 1
THE COST OF A CRIMINAL JUSTICE DEGREE

Managing the wide range of human emotions and thriving under pressure are extremely difficult challenges for law enforcement professionals.

Secure Employment in a Challenging Field.

We are actively seeking law enforcement warriors. Are you the type of champion that can help the United States avoid the same devastation and fate as the Roman Empire? It is my long-term intention that this book will ultimately assist law enforcement agencies nationwide to obtain better applicants—applicants who can make a difference and also have realistic job expectations. We truly need people who are attracted to these positions to make a social impact, while recognizing the proper steps necessary to achieve their goal. Most men have thought of themselves as being the hero at least once or twice in their lives. What about you? Whether male or female, these professions do in fact offer those real-life heroic opportunities.

Yet, due largely to a lack of knowledge, it is incredibly sad to me but ironic how we in the law enforcement community routinely exclude many potentially great applicants. Because these applicants were never informed on how to best acquire the job in the first place, they did not know how to prepare. That trend should stop today for those of you willing to learn from this publication. In case you have wavered or wondered whether the industry has jobs available, please take note: the United States Department of Labor and Industry has recorded in their 2010 statistics that there are currently over 644,300 police officer jobs in this country. This does not include investigators, detectives, and police supervisors. Additionally, correctional officers are currently listed at 457,550 careers and climbing, while there are still over three million additional law enforcement jobs carried under the "Protective Services" heading.

To be clear, the purpose of this book is to guide you through the hiring selection phase for secure employment. This is a quick guide to assist you in expeditiously obtaining a career. Every effort has been made to focus on tried-and-true essential information that will keep your budget and affordability in mind. Get busy reading for a cost-effective career education.

Today's audience includes not only the high school students, young persons in college; including those already enrolled in a criminal justice degree program, but also a target audience in the military service members who have some of the prerequisite training and experience to become excellent law enforcement candidates. Veterans are among my personal favorites as ideal applicants. Unfortunately, this group is often overlooked during recruitment by many departments simply due to a lack of college credits. Many young people from all backgrounds also get excluded for common minor lifestyle choices. One of those routine problems for all viable candidates is the practice of tattooing and body piercing on visible body areas.

Additionally, in recruitment circles complaints often flourish of not enough diversity in hiring practices for ethnic minority and women applicants. Here once again I am basically stating that anyone who has not previously considered law enforcement career opportunities could immediately benefit from reading this book. Finally, any focus on high school students *and* existing veteran law enforcement to seek this knowledge is full of individual merit since both groups should be looking to increase options or excel in their professional goals.

So, essentially anyone who is eligible and motivated to apply this information herein can ultimately gain useable insight for their ideal careers.

Also, this book serves as a support aid to law enforcement agencies that generally are not sufficiently budgeted to market to prospective candidates; it is the ideal resource for exceptional follow-up career ideas for military veterans. You will also instantly discover that this book clearly draws a line in the sand on the acceptable values and the integrity needed to carry out those principles.

It is my sincere intent to save you thousands of dollars while aiding the law enforcement community in their quest to attract good people from all walks of life. The real benefits for you should be better clarity, wisdom, and the practical information necessary to secure worthwhile employment.

Useful Insight

Since knowledge is half the battle, consider these pages a solid 'Preparation 101' course overview on a new law enforcement profession. Otherwise, if you move on to obtain the criminal justice degree, instead of focusing on receiving the actual job or career, you could likely end up without the proper insight and mindset needed to obtain law enforcement work.

This will be reflected in your paycheck when you later discover that you wasted your time to become underemployed. Please do not miss the most important aspects; the knowledge and savings which are provided here for your close examination. As a working police officer and police instructor, I cannot stress the facts enough. You are not likely to be one of the selected police recruits, or the recruit of *any* law enforcement profession, if you choose to ignore the facts in this book.

All Law Enforcement Careers

When we use the common terminology "criminal justice," let us clarify that we usually do mean police work. I have never met anyone in my life who has *initially* sought out this particular degree with aspirations of having a career in something else. Despite that, many people actually do obtain very satisfying law enforcement careers after obtaining their degree, but most often it is in a non-policing agency. Rest assured, this book directly and unmistakably applies to all related law enforcement career paths. In fact, the book specifically addresses how the career choices are not a mandatory segue from the criminal justice degree programs. All references to police are, for the most part, interchangeable with corrections officers, probation, parole, etc. Consider only that you and I are getting on the same page, if you will, in terms of the references made to police in general.

During my own career, I became frustrated with the widespread crime in the streets and with my own department's obstacles to enforcement. In truth, such frustration is being felt in all neighborhoods and law enforcement agencies across the nation. Managing the range of human emotions and thriving under pressure are extremely difficult challenges for law enforcement professionals. These long-term problems pose a serious dilemma with no quick fix in sight. Currently, it involves a significant amount of our working law enforcement personnel receiving suspensions, firings, and desk-duty-type restrictions. The question then becomes, how will you cope with such physical and mental challenges?

You may think you have it figured out from watching television shows because of how smoothly everything seemingly goes. I need you to recognize though, that even the reality shows fail to realistically depict all the issues. Frankly the editing process has to fit a show into an hour with commercials. Editing cuts out all the bad unusable information that is, in essence, *real life*; all the while still creating a captivating and entertaining show that is compelling to watch. These relevant and *real life* issues in law enforcement go largely unaddressed, but we will be discussing them here. You will need to graduate to the kind of strategic thinking that focuses on getting results for successful employment and nothing else.

In preparing to write this book, I attempted to identify the most important issues that must be examined. Simply put - choosing a career path to law enforcement requires serious preparation, practical planning, and an honest self-evaluation. After years of diligent work experience, which also included reviewing national law enforcement standards and challenges; I have pared the discipline down into a self-help book designed for aspiring law enforcement professionals to absolutely:

1. Save money and time;
2. Learn many of the unwritten and necessary requirements for the purpose of actually getting hired in a preferred position with a desirable agency;
3. Increase your individual knowledge base to become that worthy applicant through understanding the facets of the job, which includes identifying the characteristics, qualities, and requirements in detail before you apply.

You will then be far less likely to be denied or passed over in the recruitment process, which currently routinely occurs. This prevents a self-defeating end result when you become relegated to employment as an underpaid security guard, or unrelated job in a different field, with a criminal justice degree.

Congratulations on Your Wise Decision!

Consider this purchase your ultimate career conflict resolution management tool. I am confident that in acquiring this book you have made a worthwhile investment in your future.

When, and if you do move forward on this career path, congratulate yourself on what will no doubt be an exhilarating journey into a law enforcement career. We are definitely not going out of business you know! And law enforcement could really use your help, life experience and the commitment to public service. This is a career choice filled with rich, meaningful, and humbling experiences. Some of the most exceptional people in life work in law enforcement.

At sixteen, my life was heading down a dark path. My family had lost our home and I was a ward of the court. This essentially meant that the County of Allegheny in Pittsburgh became my legal guardian. I was placed into a residential group home along with forty or so other adjudicated dependent youths. Each of us suffered from little or no direction at one time or another. Such lack of direction constitutes the most common teenage phenomenon in this country. In contrast, with adequate parenting or adult direction (as you might know), a young person can get some serious time-saving or life-saving guidelines (though that has yet to bear fruit for my sons; hence, my own frustrated dedication to them). We all have free will and problems yet to be worked out. In his television show skit, "How Not to Get Your Ass Kicked by the Police," Chris Rock jokes, "I would not do that shit if I were you." Today, with liability-based mandates and polygraph testing, I would likely never have received the opportunity to become a police officer because I was, in fact, a troubled youth (liability) and a ward of the court.

A year later, after my mother found a home to rent, I experienced some brief home stability when I was returned to her care. There, I lived with my family, which then included my mother, two brothers, and two sisters. Shortly after my return that home life was again shattered when my estranged father, who lived in the same neighborhood, suddenly died from lymphoma cancer. Though we did not get along, and rarely spoke prior to his death, to this day, I miss him terribly. As a young man, I was struggling to find my place in life by putting up a front with a "mask of false bravado" to establish credibility in my neighborhood streets. It wasn't until I was in police work that I would come to find my place and my credibility or suitability.

The law enforcement community offers a tremendous opportunity to secure a fantastic career while doing awesome things. In life—no matter what option you choose for success—all you really need is a dream—a plan. Of course, burning passion and the desire to achieve something doesn't hurt either. That plan, that passion, and the results, must become a notion of progress; otherwise, you are apt to fall for anything, especially if you associate with the wrong people. In successful professional circles, it's simply called focus. Without it, you will get lost in the shuffle and end up somewhere you never expected. Much like the kids you probably know, or have heard of, who unexpectedly have died from drugs, alcohol, or drinking and driving.

I would like you to adopt laser focus. We all could use some motivation from time to time. Think about losing a fight or having someone forcing a pillow over your face. It is time to fight back and jump up to where you hope to go. From there, you should never stop moving.

Despite life's pitfalls and disappointments, forging ahead will always be better than gold or a house filled with riches. Embracing the trials and tribulations of your troubles (strife) will give you something greater—perseverance.

These are well learned lessons on the career path of law enforcement. I am simply saying that, though pain is a heavy burden, perseverance brings undeniable strength, wisdom, and understanding.

Character is ultimately what we in law enforcement are seeking, and it directly applies to all facets of life. The pages in this book are frothing with examples of strong character. The lessons, common sense, and real world applications that build such character will aid anyone, no matter from what walk of life, when seeking the higher calling of a career in law enforcement.

Funding Your Future Right Now

If you bought this book to explore this field or you are already enrolled in a criminal justice program, then you at least *think* you want a job in law enforcement. My aim is to tell you exactly what to do to get your career moving. So, for right now, let us begin under the assumption that you have, in fact, already enrolled or at least decided on a school. Whether a technical school, college, or university, there is one resounding question you must address— How will you pay for your education? With that in mind, what funding sources have you investigated?

No More Wasting Time and Money

As with many other college students, you are likely wasting money and time. Although you may be eligible for grants or scholarships for certain sought-after degrees, there are fewer opportunities in the criminal justice or criminology disciplines. Even if it were the case, most of these grant opportunities aren't made available through public knowledge. So, although it would be awesome to get a grant and save a ton of money, why not formulate a plan to save a large sum of money now by obtaining the job you desire sooner??

The question of funding sources ultimately deserves mention in order to direct your thoughts as to how much you are actually spending — or wasting. Furthermore, it once again reinforces the reasons I wrote this book; to save you, or your parents, literally thousands of dollars and to help you attain your desired career much faster.

It is my sincere hope that gaining meaningful employment is important to you. This does not include a temporary job. When I was twenty-three years old, I became a corrections officer for the Pennsylvania Department of Corrections. My starting salary in 1993 was $18,300; considered a respectable wage at that time. As a prison guard at Graterford (or, "the Fort," as some called it), I considered myself very fortunate. Back then, it was the fourth largest penitentiary in the country. The prison was a city in itself, located in Montgomery County, near Philadelphia. There we housed approximately 4,200 male inmates, almost twice the structured capacity, and many of whom were considered the worst-of –the-worst from a prone-to-violence perspective. I worked there one year and five months.

During that time, I saw extreme violence and death. In the short time I worked there, two guards died of drug overdoses and two additional guards were arrested in criminal stings. I personally experienced many hostile verbal and physical exchanges against myself and other employees, including the witnessing of a man being stabbed in the chest multiple times with a half-pair of large industrial scissors. Guards and civilian employees are subject to scrutiny, including complete strip searches upon entrance for your shift. There were a few strip searches on me, and worse yet, were several more uncomfortable, embarrassing, or inappropriate sexual contact exposures with inmate visitors in the approved visitor's room. Such examples include being in a visiting room with hundreds of people and kids running around and having to approach women and say things such as, "Ma'am, could you release his penis, please?" Additionally an inmate once struck me over the head with a wooden club when I intervened in an assault on a guard and another inmate. I suffered what in street slang is known as a "splitting of my wig," which luckily only caused some swelling and minor bleeding. For the most part, I got out of "the Fort" unscathed.

These are examples of why law enforcement officers are paid a somewhat decent wage. Until that point in my life, I had worked a lot harder for much less. Some of the many odd jobs I worked included carrying shingles up a ladder all day as a roofing laborer; and concrete pouring that required me to push around heavy wheel barrel of wet cement. I had even joined the American norm of working as a sandwich maker at Arby's Restaurant, where the manager often screamed at me. I also worked as a dishwasher, cleaning huge pots and pans for a local catering service. There are too many other jobs to mention here, but the most challenging of all was the United States Army Basic & Job Training program.

Of course, my own law enforcement career has made the biggest significant lasting impression. While in contrast, my twenty-year-old son tried two quick fast-food industry jobs but now goes to school for criminal justice (as of 2011-2012 he dropped out academically and is currently working as a dishwasher). Additionally, my eighteen-year-old son has yet to decide on a career path as I write this (he was a Taco Bell employee and in 2012, was a K-Mart employee). I, on the other hand, have consistently worked since the age of twelve. Their decision to wait is common in our society and, I believe, a serious mistake. *Life is work.* It is acceptable to work at it smartly, but it is not okay to be on constant extended breaks. Especially, if you are playing the video game, "Call of Duty," when off duty and unemployed or underemployed.

A recent example is on New Year's Eve, 2012-13, while working in a uniformed patrol capacity, I responded to a verbal domestic incident where a twenty-something, self-described "gamer" was giving his girlfriend's mother "lip" (drunk and swearing) while he lived in her house unemployed; drinking, playing video games, and sitting around the house with his two young kids. Very common and nothing short of amazing (No worries, I set him straight verbally!).

Focus

If you are a young person seeking a law enforcement career, I invite you to read this book in its entirety. If you are in high school or under military obligation, take the time to plan your future. The last thing you want to be doing years later is writing out a monthly student loan repayment check right before you race off to work at your second job!

Clarify the Career You Want

In the event that you are about to graduate, or have graduated, from a law enforcement degree program, complete this quick formula regardless, at least for the visual simplicity it will render in clarifying your new career. Allow me to logically explain with some essential facts. When you choose a school and enroll in a program, here's how you should price it out; the basic formula in determining the total price to be paid for your degree in dollars is as follows:

Based on what you know, one semester will cost you? $_____

(Write it out now in the book or on a piece of paper. Even if you are guesstimating, it will prove to be valuable to your decision making process).

Add what you know, including the cost of a college credit at your proposed or existing school, or the bill you received thus far.

Two semesters per year costs $_____

Are you enrolled, or considering, a two-year associate's degree or a four-year bachelor's degree? Circle one: Two-year degree or Four-year degree

Add up your semesters in a total dollar amount format: $_____

You Do Not Need to Go into Debt

This is the *base price* you must pay in dollars presumably to obtain the knowledge required to attain your law enforcement career. In reality; however, it is an unnecessary step. The dollar amount calculated so far excludes the time invested. What is your time worth, by the way? How do you rate the energy and time expended to study, listen, read, comprehend, and research all your class activities or projects? As a police instructor and state trooper I earn approximately forty dollars per hour. Additionally, I have earned several thousand dollars for speaking engagements. Forty dollars an hour is generally on the high-end extreme for an hourly police wage. You will earn far less if you fail to pay attention, and yet, the dangers will be just as costly.

Do Not Buy the Dream. Create Your Own.

At this point, I would like to mention the philosophy of "Selling the Dream," which conceptually means to avoid being deceived by your curriculum. We will discuss this in Chapter 4, so please savor that thought for now. Until then, let us get back to what your career choice investment can cost you. That way I can guide you through the savings and a career track with a practical roadmap. The following are the additional related costs that are most often overlooked:

Travel costs, weekly or monthly in parking or bus fees $_____
Meals (7 days/week or by semester total) $_____
Housing (9 months/year or yearly) $_____
Books (12 or 18 credits average semester) $ _____
Miscellaneous (copies, papers, parking tickets, supplies, fees, etc.)
$ _____
Total: $_____

Compare these costs annually over the length of time it takes to obtain a degree.

What Do You Really Want?

Far too many people think law enforcement sounds great. When I joined the United States Army Reserves, I became a ground surveillance radar operator. I can still hear my Staff Sergeant recruiter now, "It's exactly like police work, just like the Military Police." Um, yeah… in fact, it was not at all as he explained. Imagine that. The point is, you should take the time to talk to the working professionals in your chosen field if, and when, that is possible. These people will give you insights and perspectives that you would otherwise not have considered. Just for the record, that is what is happening exactly right now in this book. So, with the above financial totals in mind, are you just fooling around enjoying the college experience, or do you (or your parents) truly want to save some money and time?

Make It Affordable

Either way is fine. It is okay to change your elected course major and to enjoy the college experience. However, once you know for certain what your focus is, you can determine, at least, a rough draft on the price tag (or the sale) of your future options.

Planning with the Facts

It's high time for us to work together on saving you dollars. Determine exactly how to make it more affordable. Simply put at this point—at least in my mind—you bought the book, so you have clarified your intentions already, or at least, just for now. I have pledged to provide you with the very best way to <u>meaningful employment</u> and financial savings on your law enforcement career track. Obviously, financial options should require identifying your eligibility to specifically match funding sources. For the most part, such information is outside the scope of my expertise or area of focus in this publication. So it is not my "department" if you will; but consider the following relevant financial issues / avenues:

- What are your grades, GPA, or SAT scores?
- Does your credit union, church, diocese, etc. offer loans, scholarships, or grants?
- Do you qualify for school discounts for minority applicants or *any* discounts for specific programs relative to your declared major or interests?
- Do you have any interest in volunteer or work opportunities at the school; or national organizations which offer tuition assistance such as the Peace Corp, Job Corp., etc.?

- Do you or your parents belong to any civic groups, unions, associations, or other organizations that offer scholarships, subsidies, etc.?

In the event that you are truly clear that law enforcement is your chosen field, you need preparation. An ideal daily regimen or daily schedule should look like this:

- Some form of physical activity;
- Research on individual agency requirements;
- A list or resume of verifiable *or* documented employment *or* volunteer work through a non-profit organization;
- A prepared, solid list of character and credit references.

Declare a New Major

To review any and all potential savings, a student must / should measure options against the bottom-line costs; regardless of what program is chosen. It is also a smart idea to identify and compare any state funding and apply those monies according to your income guidelines.

I strongly suggest looking into these funding sources when declaring a new major with law enforcement (criminal justice) or (criminology) as a minor, at the very best. Chapter 2 begins with the hard facts as to why. This should be an immediate switch for any interested party.

Key point of this chapter: *The criminal justice degree is expensive.*

Chapter 2
ARE YOU THE VICTIM
OF A CRIME?

The objective of law enforcement remains unchanged—to secure an out-of-control situation.

Why Criminal Justice?

Although we are not going to revisit funding, I have laid the foundation for some significant financial considerations which we will continue to build on. In the meantime, consider the following question: Why do you want, or why have you chosen, a criminal justice career program in the first place? My question is legitimate and sincere. I am currently entering into my eighteenth year as a veteran police officer. That does not include my one year and five months as a state corrections officer at one of the largest prisons in the country. It also does not include my ten years in the U.S. Army Reserves, including a deployment to Bosnia, and numerous training exercises around the world.

Honorable not Glamorous

I have frequently told audiences, "I'm happy to be here and proud to serve." Yet, it is not a happy job. It is definitely honorable, but it is not glamorous, and though incredibly frustrating at times, it is deeply rewarding. Rarely is the profession, as it is sensationally portrayed on television. Have you ever been in a true knock-down, drag-out fight? During Army Basic Training in Fort Dix, New Jersey, a guy from Cleveland Heights beat me up so bad that I could not open my mouth for three days. I had to force very small pieces of food into my mouth just to eat while fellow soldiers made fun of me. It was mostly a three-day liquid diet. I had thirteen stitches sewn in my head without a numbing agent by an intern doctor who learned for the first time on my scalp. The Cleveland aggressor repeatedly kicked me in the face, head, and ribs with his Army boots. This violent encounter was a sanctioned dispute over marching too slow. The feud between our two platoons occurred on a march over several miles while carrying fully loaded rucksacks (backpacks, basically). We fought in the classroom in the evening, back at our barracks, without gear on. I think it was the first time Cleveland ever beat Pittsburgh at anything! I was sorry to let the Steel City of Champions down. (Half joking Cleveland fans; do not be mad because we are great. You still have the Rock and Roll Hall of fame).

Now, I want you to imagine being a police officer wearing heavy restrictive equipment. Do you know how it feels to roll around carrying an extra twenty-five pounds to the point of exhaustion? Yes, it is very uncomfortable, and as fate would have it, I know that discomfort, as well. How my Retired Sergeant Calvin maintained the smile he kept in this profession is too rare to mention, and it is something that might make him personally eligible for sainthood. In March 2012, a member of my department shot and killed a man who had beat him with a metal flashlight. The officer received thirty-six *staples* to repair his skull. The local newspaper reported that allegedly the officer was attacked?! http://www.publicopiniononline.com/policelog/ci_20129326/turnpike-troooper-was-attacked-by-dog-beaten-head http://www.baltimoresun.com/explore/howard/news/crime/ph-ho-cf-glances-trooper-fatal-shooting-0315-20120307,0,6411315.story

Violent Encounters and Lawsuits

The last time I got sued was 2007. I vividly remember being questioned on cross-examination by the defense attorney. "Sir, did you punch my client?" To the horror of the Assistant District Attorney, I answered, "Repeatedly, in the face, head, and ribs." The difference between the Army incident and the police case is big. In the Army, I was defending myself and my platoon's honor over virtually nothing. Although beat violently in the Army encounter, no common weapons at all were used; none were readily available or even threatened.

In the police case, I was trying to arrest a man with a gun. He was fighting at the scene of a drug deal while onlookers from a nearby bar assisted the bad guy and cheered him on. I believe the preferred chant of the evening was, "F&*$ the Police!" Every one of us had guns—the criminal, me, and my partner that day, and we also had additional multiple weapons available to the bad guy and the onlookers. These are the real instances that can cripple you with fear. That particular civil lawsuit against us was dismissed.

Expose Marketing

Successful marketing: It happens to show you in less than an hour (with commercials) how the police look cool and solve it all. Man, that new Hawaii Five-O television show is great! How about those hard bodies and kick butt fighting techniques? I could be that fit too, if I trained all the time and did not have to do my swing shift job.

In 1978, and revised up to 1995, Charles Remsberg wrote, *Tactics for Criminal Patrol, Vehicle Stops, Drug Discovery, and Officer Survival*. The book originally published by Calibre Press is a part of a three book series, (This book is now part of www.policeonebooks.com/the-complete-chuck-remsberg-set.html) and has inside the cover a photograph of a real-life, justifiable homicide that occurred between a Honolulu motorcycle cop and a criminal. I definitely consider the book the bible on *good criminal policing* and you should as well. * It is available for sworn law enforcement only. I bring this story to your attention to portray real life. Both men were shot in this incident, but thankfully, the officer survived.

A Service Job?

Nothing has changed. In the real Honolulu—and everywhere else—police officers are engaged in a dangerous, violent war. During 2011, 173 police officers were killed in the United States. It is a war that society does not necessarily wish to discuss or prefer to broadcast openly. Editor Gary Klinga of www.restassuredediting.com (who assisted me with putting this project into comprehensible English), is legitimately concerned that my vivid, honest descriptions will scare off some prospective police officers. With that in mind, remember that police work, though portrayed as cool and glamorous by the American entertainment industry, is a service job. Insofar as police personnel spend a time interacting with society's worst, or at least people at their worst, such work cannot remotely be considered glamorous.

Decisions: How Important Are They?

At one time, I was one of many officers responsible for patrolling the Parkway, the major traffic artery in the city of Pittsburgh on State Route 376. During the congested rush hour, homeless persons came up with many opportunities, scams, and cons to elicit money from stopped motorists in the area where the parkway winds through the outskirts of downtown Pittsburgh. More often than not, this amounted to the common begging for money through the use of cardboard signs or the banging on the windows of standstill, bumper-to-bumper vehicles. My personal irritation was the very rare cleaning of the windshield with dirty water, which I only observed in Pittsburgh twice. I responded to all these nuisances by aggressively removing the individuals, either verbally or forcibly. However, I learned later that I really did not want them in or on my car because they smell horrible. The fact is, these are human beings with feelings, and more often men with family, health, or mental health problems. The other plain truth is that many of them have *severe* mental health illnesses. To add to this societal problem, the jails, hospitals, shelters, and rehab centers often do not have enough room for them. In other words, it is often a lost cause to interact or interfere with their activities at all. Damn the public if they slow down and have to suffer. http://www.post-gazette.com/stories/local/neighborhoods-city/pittsburgh-homeless-people-given-a-reprieve-694780/

Basic Problem-solving

Police work is essentially a process of basic problem-solving with many complicated twists, turns and, of course, desperate circumstances. Welcome to "thinking on your feet," learning to co-exist and handling Business 101. Er, ah, I mean, "Welcome to Law Enforcement!"

Sound Practices for Gaining Law Enforcement Employment

A book like this is written to educate, possibly entertain, but definitely and almost always, to enlighten. A program, a college degree, a chance encounter—heck, even a bad relationship has; within its exchanges and circumstances, the roadmap to where you hope to go, or now maybe, where you never want to go again. Read very carefully and pay close attention. The statements and facts explained within these pages are sound practices for gaining law enforcement employment. There is no other reason for me to write this book.

Police Understanding

I am hopeful that you will gain greater insight into understanding the police mindset. Although primarily focused on the policies and practices of larger law enforcement agencies, the information provided contains the straight facts that apply exactly the same to small and rural policing entities. These facts will give you the common sense life lessons that benefit you tremendously.

Map Out a Plan

Taking the time to write out your goals will allow clarity and focus to speed up your plans. You can run circles around your friends and the competition in the progress lane. So, if you have not previously considered clear goal clarification, START WRITING NOW! I ask you to seriously reevaluate your own thought process on career planning. Take a few minutes to review the information contained within this chapter. I have some amazing and rewarding experiences to share and I hope you can make the most of your potential (A personal favorite theme and huge "ah ha" clarification point from Author Brian Tracy in his book *Goals!*).

You Are a Victim

Are you the victim of a crime if you have already enrolled in a college or university for a criminal justice discipline? If so, what would the crime be? I would like to wager a bet that you, the student, would not have a clue. You are paying for a degree presumably to secure a police or law enforcement related job. Yet, the entire focus is on theory, the accused person's rights, and forensics solvability factors. *None of these theories or focus points will help you get or keep employment.*

This makes you a victim because you are not receiving the necessary information that will help you get a career or assist you in entry level job performance. So, if you do get a law enforcement career, it is likely the result of luck, chance, opportunity, prior knowledge from a friend or family, or a clean background void of the mistakes that would otherwise exclude you.

Police Handle Business.

In 1998, I was a uniformed First Responder—"Road Dog"—as is known in street slang. At my station, we were mandated to take a mental health course. The social workers teaching the course were essentially well-meaning folks who basically provided four hours of sensitivity training. In short, very few of us paid attention and the class was an overall failure. Here is why: Police handle business. Period. In the field—out on the street in the real world—things never go textbook as in the classroom. So in theory people are generally not the best go-to-people to actually get things done (Though, they do seem to be taking over the profession).

Someone Should Be Furious.

Although specific laws, manuals, codes, and procedures vary in each state, you are still the victim of the same crime—theft! Thousands of dollars you don't even have yet are being bilked out of your future earnings as a criminal justice major. Are you too blind to see?

Jockeying for Control of an Enormous Market

Please, please get on board right now. The tide is changing. The world of academia is battling hard with technical schools, lay people, and the government. Doctorates and adjunct professors alike are jockeying for control of this enormous market. That's right—a market with millions of dollars in tuition at stake—despite the fact that this is, was, or should be, considered largely a blue collar, hands on, get your hands dirty doing work — profession. Currently, there is not one single police related law enforcement career in the country that absolutely requires a criminal justice degree at the entry level.

The Federal Bureau of Investigation *does require* a bachelor's degree, but not one in criminal justice. It should be noted, however, that as of October 2011 there is a growing trend of positions recognizing criminal justice degrees; specifically observed as preferred in the Department of Homeland Security. This preference is in regard to the new creation of the many civilian analyst jobs, which should not be confused with policing. In the future, criminal justice degrees may become a requirement as these trends grow, which is why you need to focus and examine your goals coupled with this information. So again, currently not a requirement, but preferred in some newer developing civilian jobs.

What Does the Criminal Justice Degree Really Earn?

A criminal justice degree does not earn you employment. If you are skeptical to my claim, prove me wrong. Google the Los Angeles Sheriff Department's former Basic Training Academy Reality Television Show as an excellent example. You can listen to those cadets discuss their accounting degrees. Again, we are specifically discussing obtaining law enforcement jobs, which are often referred to broadly as criminal justice careers. These are not to be confused with the civilian analyst jobs that are beginning to surface within Homeland Security; many of which do not pay as well.

It is my personal belief that disabled military veterans should be offered those analyst jobs hands down before anyone! For over ten years, we have been at war fighting in Iraq and Afghanistan. Thousands of young veterans have returned to this country missing a limb, aided with a prosthetic or otherwise injured or scarred. Many of these patriotic heroes are forced into disability but would prefer to have an active meaningful role. Any veteran who returns disabled and is capable to work should be offered those jobs over and above any graduate—every time. A veteran who is saddled with frustration, despair, lack of focus, purpose, or meaning as a result of a service disability should never be ignored.

Homeland Security exists as a result of the terrorist threat and acts of September 11, 2001. Does it make sense for our nation to offer these important jobs, which are lower paying than law enforcement, to college grads? It does not make any sense to me at all unless specific skills are identified that veterans do not possess.

Who is more knowledgeable and who would be more diligent or passionate—a veteran amputee or you with your degree? You know who I would choose, hands down, every time. Go to http://www.okshooters.com/showthread.php?143787-Tango-Mike-Mike-is-the-story-of-Green-Beret-Roy-P-Benavidez or Google other sites to watch the *Mad Arrow* film made by Mike Madero. The story title is, "Tango, Mike, Mike." It is about U.S. Army Green Beret MSgt. Roy P. Benavidez's heroic actions in Vietnam. Then, you will gain a better understanding of what I am talking about. Benavidez is a Congressional Medal of Honor recipient. His 1991 acceptance speech from President Ronald Reagan found on http://www.youtube.com/watch?v=_oUtJxE4sjs is even better. Benavidez was and remains a hero, a champion, and a great man to be followed!

Forensics

The references to forensics in the criminal justice programs completely baffle me. A career in forensics requires a science degree. At best, these course curriculums are beneficial for seasoned police investigators. Do your homework! You can have a business degree and be good to go for a law enforcement career! Why? Keep reading. The fact is that you have been duped, suckered, shanghaied. You became a willing victim of the television and entertainment industry.

Warrior Mindset

("Warrior Mindset" is a coined phrase and book by Dr. Michael Asken—with Ret. Colonel David Grossman who is the authority on "Bullet Proof Mind & On Killing & Combat" http://www.killology.com). Dr. M. ASKEN - http://mindsighting.com/ In the years to come, I imagine that academia will have their way and neuter the 'warrior mindset' of this profession. So, do you want to select the career before it may come under the auspices that a degree will help one to be more sensitive, understanding, and intelligent? Go read about Officer Jared Reston from Jacksonville, Florida for an idea of the kind of warrior spirit you need to develop to survive. He was shot at least six times at close range but decided to continue to fight to stop the teen gunman intent on killing him—over nothing more than getting caught for some stolen clothing. http://www.youtube.com/watch?v=ArDRg5SkuT0 In my area, there are many of these heroes. One is Clairton, Pa Police Officer James Kuzak, who was shot five times www.officerjimkuzak.com.

Another more recent seriously wounded Officer is Pittsburgh Police Officer Morgan Jenkins http://www.post-gazette.com/stories/local/neighborhoods-city/city-police-officer-remains-in-icu-after-gunfight-683294/ Do you know that out of all criminal justice graduates, only a very few actually end up working as police officers with any law enforcement agency? So, if you are seeking an analyst job, maybe you should continue your studies. But keep in mind that the decision is still clearly a poor choice since related experience still qualifies an applicant. A third is TFC. Brad WILSON http://www.wearecentralpa.com/story/fellow-state-troopers-share-update-on-trooper-bradley-wilson/d/story/LSvVHr5QcUej0O9mVPi6Fg

A Very Expensive Civics Lesson

If you learn nothing else from this little book, learn this *huge* lesson: Your life and people skills are the things that make you a police department asset. Is it your goal to help people? Would you like to make a difference?

The law enforcement officer is a public service position and, as such, is actually intended for you to be a servant of the community. Those of us in law enforcement are actually but a tiny mirror reflection of our society. That now means becoming a tiny portion of a decaying civilization.

It is not about you as a macho tough guy or gal as the television cop shows often portray. Instead the cold, silver bullet facts that freeze colder than Coors Lite beer is, in reality, *no* criminal justice degree is necessary for application or acceptance into this career field. The entire law enforcement system, including probation, parole, corrections, and police is or largely should be a hands-on, blue- collar work ethic type career. It can often become a, "get your hands dirty," line of work. If it is your career goal to obtain an administrative office job based on your education, performing desk duties after several years of service then, that could be considered an outstanding achievement long term plan. But, you will definitely not start in that capacity, so essentially, the degree has very little merit for *entry level.*

Intelligence Preferred. Values Mandated. Hands-on Necessary.

Linguists, computer gurus, martial artists, psychology majors, accountants— anyone with usable, tangible skills—are encouraged to apply for work in law enforcement. Or, you can get the degree. Learning about correctional rehabilitation or forensics in helping to solve crimes does not assist the police officer's mission at the crime scene. Yet, this type of curriculum is what is at the core of the teaching points of most criminal justice programs.

Did you ever pay attention in civics class? Awesome. You now have the essentials of criminal justice covered. Better still, take the time to go and sit through a criminal trial proceeding. You will then get a much better perspective. Or, even better yet, witness a new immigrant taking their Oath of Allegiance to this great nation. Then it will ring true and become Mr. Obvious to you. Police investigators are largely facilitators of resources and multi-taskers with a strong emphasis on details, facts, and hopefully strong interviewing skills. They are generally not persons with specialized forensic knowledge. It is a bonus, I suppose, but not a necessarily useful skill at entry level, especially if you are denied or declared ineligible as an applicant.

All People Have Rights in America, Even Criminals and Illegal Aliens! All Means All.

Treating people with respect is an essential principle taught in wholesome family values (Go rent Adam Sandler's "Mr. Deeds." You will enjoy a few laughs and it will serve you better than a Criminal Justice lecture). Recently, my cousin's mother was sentenced for a drug delivery that resulted in a death. She killed my cousin, David, by putting liquid methadone into his beer. She was permitted to take her methadone clinic dosage home for the weekend to combat her heroin addiction. As a result, she killed her son under the premise that she was helping him to "relax." However, because the intent was not murder and there was no one at the scene to prove that she "slipped a Mickey," my dear cousin is forever gone from this world and his real loving family. His mother—who never really knew him or had a relationship with him—received six to twelve months incarceration. Wow! She had a prior record gravity score of zero. They do not teach the gravity priority record scores in criminal justice and, just like the degree itself, frankly that does not matter either. In other words, the court system is not like television or the classroom.

What Does Matter Is How You Make a Difference.

So take heed: do not waste one dollar on a criminal justice degree. Consider this book as your "Intelligence report." Technical schools, colleges, and universities offering degrees in criminal justice and criminology are capitalizing on the high sensationalism of crime and the need for law enforcement in our society. But, here again, you are being sold a bill of goods. You do not need a criminal justice degree to enter law enforcement. These degrees may help you *after employment* is obtained, but not before. When it comes to career planning and job seeking, the programs do not address eligibility and the disciplines taught are not mandated employment requirements.

So again, law enforcement is not glamorous, but it can be very rewarding. Although a criminal justice associate's or bachelor's degree is close to worthless for entry level employment, it has merit if you decide you want to be a police chief, a corrections superintendent, a warden, or police instructor and alike. Then, the degree and title sounds official and prestigious next to your name. But, even with those positions, you must work your way up the promotional ladder. As a job seeker, you should be thinking entry level and how do I get hired. A criminology degree is also the same, and largely a meaningless piece of paper for a rookie officer. Your ability to pass a polygraph and a background investigation is, however; **very relevant**.

Overall, as of 2010, many city police departments require a high school diploma and no felony convictions. Check out the Memphis, TN Police Department's recruitment web page http://mpdacademy.com/requirements.php. Memphis PD recently changed their requirements and now requires fifty-four credits or two years military service. While many state agencies and townships tend to look for some college diplomas, federal agencies, such as the Federal Bureau of Investigation, again still require a bachelor's degree— in any major. Corrections careers often require a high school diploma. Requirements for security positions vary with the employers.

Despite the nationwide academic push for college credits and criminal justice degrees, law enforcement cannot find, hire, and keep qualified people. Here is exactly why: The old world values of virtue and responsibility are competing with a blameless culture and squarely losing the fight. Most importantly, no one is warning applicants on the do's and do nots of acceptable behavior. In simple terms, the public servant career path is banking on applicants to adhere to the character values of previous generations. Those values are currently under attack by our own information technological society. My department, for example for a time, excluded many potentially great applicants because they had downloaded music on the Internet, with sites such as Napster. Do you want to be one of those applicants who spent $60,000-70,000 on a criminal justice career degree only to be excluded for five dollars' worth of music? If not, then please follow along while we review.

How to Get There

Depending on your life experience, you are likely very naive about what you are about to embark upon. In my area, a local university offers a nationally recognized criminal justice degree program. The school has approximately eight professors with doctorates in the program; which also offers an advanced extended graduate degree in both criminology and criminal justice. These disciplines have partnerships that include some of the retired federal agents who actually pioneered behavioral assessments. That fact alone adds enormous creditability to the program, and personally, I remain very interested in the programs capabilities. These highly-educated academics have access to millions of dollars worth of equipment. For instance, ground-surveying radar to assist in the discovery of bodies, and other evidence. The classes offered in this discipline can be extremely useful, very interesting—and as state-of-the-art high tech options, designed to assist with crime solvability factors. As a matter of fact, one of my many goals is to reach out and partner with this school to assist local and state police officers with investigations.

But here is the enormous "elephant in the room" takeaway for you; these classes will not help you to get a job or to get a specialized position within a department. They can benefit veteran law enforcement with new perspectives, solvability factors, and intelligence. But, there are no additional monies or promotions for even these veteran officers to attend these classes *in most scenarios*. Another discouraging downside is - these college professors often have no real field experience; but will likely be considered as qualified experts and may even testify against law enforcement in court. The few that do have minimal experience sometimes paint one case as their "swan song" or they partner with a retired agent / officer with law enforcement credentials to validate their concepts, programs, and overall creditability. As many of my fellow department members have often recited to me (giving me a shot when I was working as a full time instructor), "Those who cannot fight, teach," a reality that is maybe at least a half-truth.

Thinking You Know Something

I am relatively certain that if you are in a criminal justice program, or have graduated from one, you are filled with the usual cockiness and foolishness of thinking you know something. Rest assured; you do not. Today, the police are on trial and under a microscope. If you ever become employed in the law enforcement arena, your smug arrogance will get you hurt, fired, or arrested as sure as O.J. Simpson got acquitted. To help you assimilate these facts closer to your generation, let us consider what the music rap artist and millionaire Jay-Z has to say in his song lyrics "H to the Izzo," "Beat those charges like Rocky...put your damn hands up." The facts behind the song are: Jay-Z stabbed a record producer multiple times in front of several witnesses, apparently as an objection to the sale of bootleg counterfeit compact discs. Jay-Z ultimately received nothing more than a slap on the wrist from the justice system; which means the arresting officer's case was minimized. Later Jay –Z moved on to turn the episode into a multi-million dollar hit. I guess that is poetic justice? http://bossip.com/303295/jay-z-decodes-99-problems-the-btch-was-actually-a-drug-sniffing-k-9-dog30346/

You Will Likely Be Assaulted

Those of us in law enforcement have a long, tedious, and violent road ahead. Many of you who are hired by law enforcement agencies will risk your lives in the street or on the cell block. Do not ever count on a criminal's mercy to save you in dire circumstances. If you are hired, you need to know that it may be a long time before the pendulum of violence swings the other way. In August 2012, a Clay County, West Virginia man arrested for reckless driving shot two Troopers, one Deputy Sheriff and a tow truck driver. Cpl. Marshall Bailey and Tpr. Eric Workman died and Deputy John Westfall was hospitalized. http://old.post-gazette.com/pg/12245/1258588-455.stm

I hope to educate and prepare you for those dangerous days ahead. If you have any illusions about the dangers, I recommend you go to a host of legitimate websites which can quickly verify the number of assaults and deaths on police officers. The *Officer Down Memorial* (www.odmp.org) page includes four friends with whom I had the honor to serve, as well as many others whose funerals I attended. I also recommend the F.B.I.'s *Uniformed Crime Reporting Program* (www.fbi.gov/about-us/cjis/ucr/ucr) and the F.B.I.'s *Law Enforcement Officers Killed and Assaulted Program* (www.fbi.gov/about-us/cjis/ucr/leoka) as solid verification.

Commonplace American Violence

There are numerous factors that contribute to crime in our country. But, the basic foundation that remains is primarily due to the injustice and violence that are all too commonplace in our American culture. The metropolitan areas, in particular, our poorer neighborhoods, as well as many smaller cities and rural communities, have been devoured by drug use and lawlessness. Take a walk down those streets if you dare. Or, visit the streets along the Mexican border where illegal alien violence and "drug war" epidemics have erupted into territorial warfare. It is the drug consumption that is largely draining law enforcement resources. Society's lows have currently reached an all-time high. In response, our media culture amplifies the problem as breaking news. Television programs and movies then have a tendency to focus on the actions of police officers. In the aftermath, the events that happen in split seconds are turned into months of review and debate. The media and public at-large really need to be better informed that the police *are not the reason* for crime and violence. A case in point is the shooting of Trevon Martin in Florida and the resulting resignation of the Sanford, Florida police chief, who said he was stepping down temporarily in the wake of the public outcry over the failure of the police to arrest George Zimmerman, the neighborhood watch volunteer who said his February 26, 2012 shooting of Martin was an act of self-defense. The case had racial overtones and media sensationalism which can unfortunately influence the outcome. I say unfortunately because each case should be centered on facts only. As of August 2013, we all know the verdict and the outcry. It appears to be an all-around tragedy with no winners, in my opinion, and with the police to blame.

Florida Defendant Casey Anthony's attorney was very successful in exploiting the justice system and getting off the topic of facts; (http://en.wikipedia.org/wiki/Death_of_Caylee_Anthony). The objective of law enforcement remains unchanged—to secure an out-of-control situation. Those of us in law enforcement are held to a much higher standard than the bad guys. When it comes to assaults and murder, criminal deeds receive less attention, with usually a brief newspaper paragraph about the incident or the efforts of the police officer in stopping the crime. In contrast the media's frequent sensationalism of our blameless culture, the police officer's use of any force, or even deadly force, is doubly scrutinized. If I get into a car chase with a fleeing felon who happens to sustain an injury, I am invariably blamed. As police officers, we function daily in this environment where excessive violence has ultimately become the normal form of communication on our streets.

Interacting with Underachievers

Law enforcement routinely translates to dealing with "the worst of the worst" and people who are not functioning at peak or even moderate performance levels. Once again, how sad! If you are curious about what type of people you will confront, then know that they are most often those underachievers who beat each other up, get incredibly high or intoxicated; lie, steal, cheat, and throw trash all over their neighborhood streets and houses for someone else to clean up. They are frequently those who have little respect for themselves or anyone else. Regardless of the circumstances that got them in that current situation, many—if not all—of these individuals have graduated to "zero personal responsibility." Generally, I would speculate these persons have not visited www.values.com, which includes tag lines about integrity. This "career path" often includes regular house calls to roach, rat, and feces-infested dwellings with dirty diapers, fast-food wrappers, mounds of clothing, aggressive language, and door-less refrigerators, which all generate those offensive smells to complement the visual images. No need to wonder anymore. These are, in fact, the typical human environments you will likely be dealing with on a daily basis as an officer, whether policing, checking up on your probation convict, or the corrections officer walking the tier of your cell block.

Sometimes, the culprit is poverty. Other times, it is a lack of values, despair, mental health issues, or just a purely selfish criminal mindset. Regardless of cause, the environment is still negative. Many of America's cities have declined to the point of a third world country. Whether it is Detroit or Pennsylvania's Mon Valley. But do not get me wrong. Regardless of all the factors contributing to such decline, the point is that this is the way it is and this is the working environment where you are likely to find yourself when employed.

Check your local headlines for the victims of violent crime. It is common mainstream daily news fare. Or, as I have already suggested, go sit in a courtroom at your county courthouse. You will learn, see, and be exposed to so much more in a few hours than you can ever experience in a four-year degree program that consists primarily of classes in theory. Believe me. I know they give you the smoke and mirrors. Heck, some of you may even see autopsies in your program study internships. Trust me, though. It still does not even remotely compare to real life enforcement. Policing is a lot scarier. San Diego Police Officer / Marine Combat Veteran Officer Jeremy Henwood http://www.youtube.com/watch?v=l4h_2vBVwUA

Extreme Negativity

All self-help gurus and motivational speakers talk about attitude, environment, and choices. The police officer's daily onslaught of negativity is both senseless and endless. Do not be disheartened. Welcome to your new career world, a world which usually includes job security for most of us; unless there is a budget to balance. In 2009, I did not get paid for approximately one month due to a budget shortfall. It crushed my credit rating in the aftermath for a long time. So, I strongly recommend that once you are working you enjoy your off time and try to create balance in your life in the form of hobbies and quality family time (with a savings plan!). Keep your profession in perspective by comparing what it offers in security against what it costs you in terms of negative exposure, attitude, and life expectations.

Cop Shows

Take the time to reflect and compare the negativity against the long line of police shows and dramas that depict the glamour. Check Wikipedia online to access a list of such programs (under search titles such as "police drama or crime drama shows"). I really want you to check these out because of their seemingly glamorous appeal. Just like you, I also have several personal favorites when it comes to police drama television. I have even found some serious hero and leadership traits that I would prefer to emulate: *T.J. Hooker, Dragnet, CHiPs, 21 Jumpstreet, New York Undercover, Kojak, Hill Street Blues, Law and Order, NYPD Blue.* I also like more current dramas, including *Monk, Blue Bloods, Southland, Persons of Interest, Criminal Intent, The Mentalist, Psych, Cold Case, Without a Trace, Flashpoint,* and *Justified.*

Entertainment or a Career Choice?

However, one should be extremely cautious when evaluating career choices based on entertainment. All around the world, police are engaged in life and death struggles. Most of the work has, unfortunately, become "routine." It may soon become *your* routine. To our demise, it is this routine that is most often overlooked by the courts and media as something that is part of the job. Is this what you long for and want to work toward? In 1997, I had an incredibly violent fight with a very stocky, angry man. As a result, the man received three months' incarceration. As a frustrating sidebar, the woman he beat refused to testify, and odds are she is still with him today.

A Chance for Humility

Despite such outcomes, it is still gratifying to serve and do well. It is also satisfying to be able to defend or protect yourself and others. Most importantly, the job is very humbling when you actually do serve. It is important to recognize that you will encounter many people in poor and dire circumstances who are not necessarily evil. They are people you can, and should, help. You do have a profound impact on their lives, decision-making and, ultimately, the course of their future.

However, we are not a volunteer organization. This is not Big Brothers and Sisters. I highly recommend that you consider volunteering with a reputable non-profit organization. Otherwise, get involved with a good church that has a productive outreach ministry. These choices provide peace and balance to combat the anger, frustration, stress, and pointless chaos of your career path. Here is one place to start: http://www.unitedway.org/

Decisive Missions

As human beings, we adapt to our environment, and serving a segment of the population living in despair often places you in the dragon's lair. Thus, our mission in law enforcement must be focused on control and not on social approval. Sometimes the end result or goal is the same as it is for regulatory agencies, churches, non-profits, or social services. But police work is more about containment, security, and the type of result or goal that is achieved by forced compliance when necessary. The point is, we make more adversaries / enemies than friends because we do at times force change.

Who do you think has a greater impact on the lives of the troubled poor or angry masses—the people portrayed on television, movies, and music video artists; or real-life police officers? Ironically, the masses answer is not real-life police officers. A career in law enforcement hardly equates to the "kick ass good time" it is perceived to be and is often portrayed as by the media at large. Even by the "Cops" Reality Show. This is because *law enforcement is not a reward based profession.* People do not thank you for arresting them; or for seizing their thousands of dollars in drug product.

You will never receive a letter from a convicted criminal saying, "Holy shit, Man! Thanks a lot for helping to turn my life around and getting me on the straight and narrow. This third felony conviction should be no problem. After I get out in ten years or so, I will work at a minimum wage job and get it right this time. Do me a favor Brother, and stop to check on my lady and kids for me from time to time, would you? I'm sure she will definitely wait for me.

Thanks again, Officer, for taking me to task. You are the best."

Sincerely,

Mr. Criminal.

You Cannot Be Cool in Police Work.

Police work is not like the life portrayed by Sylvester Stallone and Kurt Russell in the movie *Tango and Cash*.(I know I am showing my age). The movie implies that a police officer or detective can dress well, smell good, and be super fit. Eventually, the effects of swing shifts, long hours, no sleep, violence and the all-around negativity definitely catches up in one form or another.

Have you ever seen the reality television show where Steven Segal is a reserve police officer in Louisiana? He has put on more than a few pounds and looks much different than he did in all his movies when he was in peak physical condition. Obviously, it would be awesome if you could train all day and avoid the effects of life and aging instead of having to testify in court on your off days. In early 2012, I was in court for three weeks on a homicide trial. I was in court daily at eight o'clock in the morning, and we generally convened around six o'clock in the evening. Then I proceeded to the District Attorney's office where we prepared for the next day's testimony. Or, many nights I went out in search of witnesses to interview or subpoena. Most days were at least twelve hour days, only to get up and do it again. Sitting through and testifying at the trial is the easy part.

Several months before that trial; I testified in a motion to suppress the criminal case; where I was on the stand for over an hour while a high-priced, well-known defense attorney belittled me for destroying a full notebook and reducing my notes to a report. Nothing was mentioned about his client or his client's criminal involvement. Such is the typical deception and silliness we in policing often have to endure.

Workers Get Heavy Caseloads

Real life workers cope with heavy caseloads, years of stress, and many sleep deprieved nights. Meanwhile, television shows just get new characters and a single case to solve in an hour or less. It is of vital importance to remember that you have one life to live. Therefore, while it is a true honor to serve, do not be in such a hurry to waste your most valuable asset - You.

Adversaries

A law enforcement officer has three potential adversaries:

1. The criminal or out-of-control person at the scene, station house, or jail.
2. The police / corrections / probation administrators who at times employ and focus on liability, political correctness, and damage control. It is awkward to say the least; when you start out as a servant of the public to do well and end up as the subject or target of accusations of wrong doing.
3. The legal maneuvering of participants in the court system who can be swayed, corrupted, compromised, or biased. Meaning, as one example, Defense Attorneys who often verbally bait or attack Officers on the witness stand simply as a strategy instead of an inquiry into the truth. Also, Attorneys for the State frequently compromise by offering plea agreements for reduced jail sentences to clear their overburdened caseload; or they offer a deal to obtain a conviction on a lesser offense rather than risk a possible not guilty verdict in a trial. And, Judges are human so they can haves biases, golf buddies, or even their own political agenda.

All are equally challenging. Go rent the 1976 Clint Eastwood Dirty Harry movie, "The Enforcer." The Police Administrations today are still bound by the same liability focused mandates. The absolute bottom line is your future. Whether a police officer, corrections officer, or probation officer, you are an expendable asset as a foot soldier in the "war on crime." Do not doubt me. Why do you think all those force options are contained on an officer's belt?

Use Your Brain.

As officers we are provided with thousands of dollars' worth of good equipment and training. However, it still *remains much cheaper to bury us.* The best weapon you carry was never issued; it is located between your ears. Use it often to keep things in perspective.

Again, I encourage you to check or review the *Officer Down* website or the *Washington D.C. Police Memorial* and trust me on this one. Please research the *LEOKA* (Law Enforcement Officers Killed and Assaulted Program). The statistics should offend you and will likely blow your mind. No officer should ride alone anywhere in this day and age; yet the majority of us do for the cost effective advantage of the additional police vehicle "coverage," which simulates a sufficient uniform presence. This is typical everywhere. When I was a prison guard, there was, on average, one guard for every two hundred inmates. We all hung out together on the block, inmates and guards alike. Unlike depictions on television where the guards walk by locked-up cells. That only occurs in Restricted Housing Units, during count time, or maybe in some county facilities.

Agencies Hope to Acquire Good People

Funding in the form of grants and scholarships is available for teachers. In contrast, zero dollars are available specifically for criminal justice majors. The exception to the rule is the rare internship within programs recently established for large government agencies, such as Homeland Security. Even then, they are not paying for or seeking the criminal justice degree; and those intern opportunities are definitely few and far between. These agencies hope to acquire good people with specialized skills. They are not looking for someone who can recite the Bill of Rights. We hold these truths to be self-evident, that all criminal justice programs are the same— worthless for an entry level career. No disrespect to our country's Founding Fathers. More importantly, I especially mean no disrespect to laypersons, professors, and law enforcement instructors who are working hard to bring meaningful classroom projects, concepts, and experiences to the specific program disciplines they serve.

The reason for this book and the dialogue within is specifically to address the pitfalls these degree programs have created. Simply put, the college market implies that a person who graduates will be a more desirable law enforcement candidate. Such a claim is one hundred percent false. Recently when I was instructing a municipal police academy class; one of the female students discussed the benefits of her criminology degree. I seek to educate instead of offending or demoralizing someone. We all agree there is a real world benefit to any education. Nonetheless, after telling us about all her neat volunteer projects and interactive studies, she failed to recognize her seating placement. Her degree did not qualify her for anything extra. She sat with everyone else in the classroom who did not have that degree and she will get no extra pay for her degree once she gains employment. Furthermore she has multiple tattoos, one specifically on the left wrist as a bracelet. This tattoo alone may disqualify her from employment at many law enforcement agencies. Amazingly, she already knows this, but since she has been indoctrinated into believing the degree has value; it is not really registering in her mind. This is the reason I wrote this book! These issues infuriate me. It is just plain wrong to allow people to assume they can secure employment through these degree programs only to discover you will be turned down. I also instructed a previous class where a trainee's arm now makes him appear to be a burn victim. He was required to remove all his visible tattoos immediately. Because he had to buy over the counter chemicals at the last minute, he severely damaged his skin.

Key Chapter Point: *You may not actually want this career choice for the right reasons.*

38

Chapter 3
START AN INVESTIGATION

Beware of the sales pitch rhetoric before making a serious decision on which career path you want to take.

Support the Elements of the Crime against You

Now is the right time to do your own investigation. Weigh the gravity of my words for yourself. Measure them against a reasonable standard. In police investigations there is something called the "elements of the offense" or the "elements of the crime." A straightforward example in simplest terms is that in the case of burglary you must have someone breaking into your home or into your business to satisfy the elements of this crime; and then you need to prove the intent of the crime.

Any relative proof that a structure was entered is one of the key elements: a pry mark, a broken window, a ski mask, and any missing items. In the case of an assault on a person, you as the investigator need physical contact or the threat of physical contact. Without any elements you have no crime. This is also where the saying "no victim, no crime" is born. Consider that I do not hate people committing crimes; but I absolutely despise not only what they are doing to themselves but also what they do to the innocent persons in their self-destructive path.

Corpus delicti

Now, transfer this new concept for you as a student. If you are currently enrolled in a criminal justice degree program, you may have a professor that discusses the root of these concepts by dropping some Latin terminology on you. For example, the term *corpus delicti* (the body of the crime) may be discussed in the classroom. It sounds so official, but in reality, who cares? Does it qualify or prepare you for employment? That is my point. In the quest for a degree, a student is not even getting the basic concepts of criminal elements to complete routine investigations. Better yet, most students will not even retain the jargon that is spouted off in the classroom. Bottom line, allow me to prove the elements of this crime to you. *It is the case of get your job now and a different degree later.* The body of the crime is the fact that you are paying for something that gives you absolutely *no advantage* over someone who does not have the degree. When police work leads to an arrest it is the result of proving the elements. When the case moves to the courtroom, it is all about strategy. We in law enforcement hope the truth is exposed in the process. But this little known fact is much like the truth about what is required to obtain this career.

Diversify and Make Yourself More Marketable.

And so, I present the following factual evidence to support the elements of the crime committed against you as a student:

1. A criminal justice degree is not required anywhere. Do not confuse this with some agencies which require *some* college course credits. *The distinction is that the credits can be in any discipline.*
2. You still must go to a police academy or accredited qualifying school in your respective state to meet the legal requirements of a career as a sworn officer. This is a basic training program.
3. The police academy's training is much different than the criminal justice program. With a focus that will concentrate on physical readiness, firearms proficiency, legal comprehension, and academic testing for law and case law, and then some degree of your personal adaptability or mental suitability. This is most often designed in a regimented paramilitary training atmosphere that also includes psychological testing.

The Facts

These facts are in sharp contrast to the theory of criminal justice program practices which tend to focus on the purpose of jailing, people's rights or advanced policing solvability factors with forensics. The website www. criminaljusticeusa.com is efficient and represents itself to be educating would-be law enforcement professionals. The basic job descriptions on the lower left corner of the home page could assist the reader with a better understanding of potential career duties. What is seriously lacking, however, is any proven research or fact to support the assertion that "a criminal justice degree is preferred." Furthermore, not one actual police department link or law enforcement agency is listed. Of course the direct links to "the best criminal justice programs" are provided. I would speculate that either the site owner / creator is a school affiliate, or the schools themselves have created this marketing effort. Either way, it is a very professional and informative site. (As of January 2013, www.criminaljusticeusa.com has added an 'About' page and advises it is noncommercial). But, when you are seeking a job or career, you generally apply to the potential employer. Do you hear what I am screaming at you?

The Military: Best and Cheapest

The closest comparison to law enforcement is the military. Go and join. Instead of the degree that you pay for and spend years to acquire, the military pays you. Here is a clue! Universities and colleges value experience in military service by providing the student with credits. This in turn, further qualifies you for those departments and agencies which require an associate's degree or the equivalent. At least check out the ROTC program at your current school. I recognize that many people do not want to surrender their weekends. Others do not want to associate with people who are not cool in their eyes. However, many law enforcement jobs offer ten military preference points for test taking applicants. That means that you get ten additional points over and above all non-military applicants for your military service efforts. So, do you really want this career or not?

Structure and Discipline

In all probability, law enforcement will continue to assume some form of a paramilitary model. Therefore, as an officer, you must follow orders because there is a chain of command and a regimented process (Despite my background I struggle with this at times and, to a degree, I remain anti-establishment in a professional tongue-in-cheek way). Furthermore, if you don't like guns and violence this may not be a good career move for you. Law enforcement and the military are extremely diverse in the opportunities and the possibilities that exist in job descriptions, training, and travel. Obviously, there are big distinctions but far too many similarities to dismiss.

The Mission

Military and law enforcement have one essential purpose in common: *support of the mission.*

In law enforcement, the mission translates to policing, including a basic patrolling function as a uniformed first responder. In the military, the mission often means combat training preparation and then conducting training drills related to your individual job, sometimes geared around occupying an area by force. So all police officers, regardless of their specific job, may still be first responders, and all military service members may still be called upon to defend regardless of position.

Any Branch of Service Is Suitable.

In review, the military actually pays you to meet most law enforcement job requirements. Any branch of military service will provide free training and often even financial opportunities for enlistment bonuses in exchange for your time. Remember in Chapter 1 when we discussed what your time is worth? As a capable person who obtains a steady paycheck with free housing, health care benefits and life insurance, doesn't that seem far better than taking out student loans? At least in my mind it does, especially if law enforcement is your goal and if you have a sincere wish to serve and protect. Obviously the term "free" means in exchange for your time.

Dangerous Work

Although there is nothing wrong with wanting to seek secure employment, both the military and law enforcement actually ask much more of you. You are asked to take an oath that you are expected to uphold. You are expected to perform extremely dangerous work. In the event that you are less than honorable and have no intentions of <u>honoring</u> the commitment, the odds to survive might still go against you. We literally seek out trouble, so the those odds definitely increase. You work with weapons and dangerous equipment in real-life, high-stress situations. Many a man has died in training exercises or from friendly fire. The unfortunate death of Corporal Pat Tillman, Army Ranger and NFL star, epitomizes the extreme danger in such friendly fire. Please learn more about this great man and American hero at: <u>http://www.pattillmanfoundation.org</u>. Obviously, the number of such fatalities is incredibly smaller compared to those suffered from enemy fire during combat. Yet, that is of no comfort to families or loved ones. So, you should know that it does happen and it is a sobering reminder of both the responsibility and the dangers inherent in this kind of service; just like law enforcement.

Applying Additional Points

Not only is serving your country an extremely valuable and honorable experience, but you also receive veteran points for military service. The points count over and above your initial law enforcement test score for most agencies which legally permit additional consideration. Thus, you benefit from well-deserved, preferential treatment for a veteran's option, if you will. Over and above the opportunity to garner points, most of your basic training experience counts toward your elective credits at many universities and colleges.

Recognizing Military Service

If you are a veteran who has served in any branch in an active duty capacity, including service as a current or former enlisted member of a Reservist or National Guard Unit, you are eligible to receive *free* college credits. In the event that you are seeking employment with a law enforcement agency that now requires some college course credits, these credits give you a significant head start.

Vast Opportunities

If you are a young person, you really should not overlook the vast job opportunities that the military offers. Do some homework. You can enlist in the Army band, be a Coast Guard diver, move satellites with the Air Force, become a truck driver in the Marines, or direct planes on a Navy aircraft carrier. There are hundreds— if not thousands—of possibilities in between. But never forget that at its core, military service is designed for the defense of this great nation. Therefore, the fact remains that you may get called upon to serve on active duty here in America or quite possibly abroad. Just like police work, you will serve. That likely means such things as late nights in the pouring rain—in the ocean or a foxhole. In police work that might mean twelve hours at a bloody crime scene or twelve hour shifts on the prison block during a lockdown as a corrections officer.

Accountability Is a Good Thing.

So, to be sure, discipline and accountability are good values to practice when you do move on to begin your law enforcement career. That essentially is what the profession entails in its simplest form. As a police officer, you are the only one holding people in this society accountable in a rapidly changing and "it's not my fault" world. As you digest our conversation, evaluate if the military is right for you. Consider that here is what the military in any branch again offers you upon enlistment:

- A guaranteed paycheck;
- Health insurance;
- Dental insurance;
- Life insurance;
- Potential / possible retirement as a career;
- Job / career training and experience;

THE MYTH ABOUT CRIMINAL JUSTICE DEGREES

- Physical readiness / fitness;
- Housing;
- Discount shopping / duty free (tax free) stuff;
- Travel;
- Personal accountability; and
- A chance to work toward your individual full potential.

Challenges and Misconceptions

Any misconceptions or illusions about military service will be quickly dispelled upon entering a controlled, structured environment. Structure is the military's baseline and something in absolute stark contrast to today's blameless culture. In Fort Dix, New Jersey, my 382-man company completed a fourteen mile rucksack march. That means toting full, heavy packs of equipment while carrying an M16 rifle at port arms (chest high). The march was conducted in deep sand. Two hours after our 'lights out' return, we were doing pushups in our boxer shorts outside in the cold. Suffice to say, I did not enjoy it much, but adversity builds character. The marches at Fort Huachuca, Arizona, were even tougher. That iron has aided me in my job performance as a police officer many times in the years that followed.

Your Mettle Will Be Tested.

Structure often creates the focus and organizational skills necessary for success and personal achievement. Seeing any mission through to its completion generates a deep feeling of accomplishment. Military missions are usually group oriented but often take on the sense of personal achievement and growth. Make no mistake: the military will test your mettle and the limits of your capabilities; all the while asking you to become personally responsible.

Accountability 101

The thought process of, *if it has to be, then it's up to me,* means learning to understand authority, hierarchy, and the basic principles of respect and leadership. These are some of the key ingredients to successfully serving in the military. In truth, these "ingredients" also constitute the basic key traits necessary to any successful individual achievement. Again, such essential leadership traits also apply to police work. One of the biggest setbacks in military and law enforcement service is the potential to work for incompetent space wasters. While I have had the distinct displeasure to have served under such people, I have also worked for some incredible leaders. Sometimes it means working with someone whom you really dislike or with someone you might have a personality conflict with. Many times in those circumstances, you grow to despise their views due in part to the attitudes, beliefs, or the perceived incompetence they demonstrate. But these are encounters to be expected in the course of a career and serve as painful enduring life lessons.

Roll with the Punches

I once transferred to a police station in my home county / neighborhood. I foolishly thought that I would now at last have some welcome stability in my personal life with a chance to spend more time with my sons. My new supervisor, however, had a different agenda when she wrote me up eleven times for questionable and petty field regulation infractions. It took me a little while before I finally got the message that I was not welcome. I then realized that I should transfer to another location. I am stubborn and that was well after she told me she did not want me in her unit. Apparently, this unit was not going to be my home station! The experience was more of a life lesson than a paramilitary phenomenon. In other words, personality conflicts, egotistical supervision, and incompetence all exist and co-exist with you in any workplace. Your ability to adapt and get along with people is an extremely useful mindset to develop. Military service and police work provide such a necessary mindset every day simply through the acceptance of that personal responsibility.

High Achievers

Overall, the military is filled with large numbers of high achievers and a fair number of deadbeats sprinkled in. To appreciate a high achiever, go to http://www.youtube.com/watch?v=50RFJfUzNsY and watch "The Sal Giunta Story." There are numerous videos for this newer Medal of Honor awarded veteran, but you definitely want the unpolished, not politically correct version which includes his conversation on working at Subway as a sandwich artist. Giunta has a new book out: *Living with Honor,* available at http://www.amazon.com/Living-Honor-Memoir-Sal-Giunta/dp/1451691467. He is now also a sought after speaker. I have already mentioned another very high achiever, Roy Benavidez. His achievements should inspire you and resurrect your belief in your fellow man. He was a great American—also referred to as a great Mexican-American.

So rest assured if you decide on the military, law enforcement, or both, it is pretty much a no brainer and goes without saying. Be prepared to work with some incredible leaders and a sizeable number of fools. They call it life. MSG Paul Howe, U.S. Army Retired, addresses this masterfully in his book, *Leadership and Training for The Fight.* (http://www.amazon.com/Leadership-Training-Fight-Thoughts-Operations/dp/1420889508). Howe was one of the main U.S. Army Delta members in the real events depicted in the movie Black Hawk Down.

Focus on Your Contributions

If the branches of service spark your interest and you are considering the military; take a few moments to review your health status and personal beliefs. First, check to see if you have any of the following physical restrictions or health issues:

- Heart murmurs;
- Asthma;
- Severe food allergies;
- Medicine allergies;
- Vision problems;
- Bone or muscle injuries or previous surgeries; or
- Diseases or diagnoses that would prevent you from serving.

I know about these matters because I joined with some of these physical conditions. It made for more than a few rough days! To be specific, I enlisted with severe asthma. It resulted in two emergency room visits in Basic Training. Today, most branches of service rigorously screen asthmatics. Next, do you have any moral, ethical, or religious objections that would prevent you from serving in the military? My department currently has an officer who openly claims he cannot shoot another human being. He could be occupationally misplaced because, though shooting another person is never a goal, it is an appropriate response to stop the dangerous actions of a violent assailant. Once such moral objections are answered, you should be able to make a general self-awareness evaluation of your personality and the traits that are suitable for service. Are you capable of teamwork, leadership development and following simple directions? At entry level these are commonplace daily orders and requirements that must be carried out. Most of those orders and requirements identify and mold the key leadership traits that will become essential to your law enforcement work needs.

The Ideal Law Enforcement Officer
Leadership Traits:

- Leads by example
- Functions well in a group
- Functions well independently
- Works well and effectively independently without supervision
- Trustworthy
- Reliable
- Decisive
- Good listener
- Empathetic
- Strong physically and mentally

Misconceptions and Relevance
A very common misconception is that military service means fighting and shooting people. Although it can be a big part of military operations and

should always be considered as a real possibility, it is much the same as crime on America's streets. It really depends on where you are and what you are doing.

In war, the rules of engagement are most often quite different than in police work. However, the rules of engagement in police work continue to become more warlike while the military continually engages in humanitarian or peacekeeping missions that are becoming police- like missions all over the world.

In 1999, I was deployed to Bosnia and attached to the U.S. Army 10th Mountain Division as an E-5 Sergeant Army Reservist. We maintained an occupied presence at Camp Eagle with soldiers from several different countries. Some of our soldier units actually provided patrols in the city of Tuzla outside of the razor wire guarded base. My support unit did not actively engage the factions in any military actions during my deployment. However, on guard duty, I did see citizens shooting in the air with guns on a few occasions outside of the wire. I also witnessed several small children navigate the razor wire to beg; often for a Pepsi; with the chant, "Gimmie me Pepsi." When we did go to town, the houses on the way were all riddled with giant holes from mortar rounds in the dead of winter. Every house was occupied though regardless of its condition.

No "Cop-outs"

No matter what your profession, there is always the risk of death. Death is imminent in life. Many convenience store clerks are robbed, beaten, and shot. Also, take for example, the unfortunate set of circumstances that occurred one night for the United States Army Reserve soldiers of the 14th Quartermaster Water Purification Unit of Greensburg, Pennsylvania. Several of these soldiers were killed by a Scud missile fired during the first Iraq War while they played cards off-duty in a tent while serving in Saudi Arabia. http://en.wikipedia.org/wiki/14th_Quartermaster_Detachment. The thousands of police on the *Officer Down* web page also serve as humbling reminders of the dangers of police work. Approximately 150 officers are killed annually while on duty in the United States each year.

I have recommended www.odmp.com. (*Officer Down Memorial Page*) because history repeats itself. You will discover that some of the police officers were victims of violence that took place near your home. Death occurs in everyday civilian life. The numbers of victims of car crashes, work accidents, and violent crime are easy to reduce to cold statistics. But I want you to clearly understand that in law enforcement you will be encountering many deadly circumstances up close and personal—daily.

Graphic Death and Violence

The sight of victims of violence forever changes you and your outlook on life. One of my first encounters with police duty violence was witnessing a beautiful young woman take her last breath. I had maybe sixty-five days on the street and I had already experienced death repeatedly; but this was my first time watching it up close as it happened. She had just broken up with her boyfriend. He felt she could not be with anyone else, and so he shot her in the face. I stayed with her until the ambulance personnel arrived. As she choked on her own blood and gasped for breath, I told her she would be all right. It was, in fact, not all right and would never be again for her family, her young son or the man she had just met who was also murdered upstairs. She died in front of me gurgling on her own blood with one eye staring at me while ambulance personnel worked in vain to save her.

Training and Physical Readiness

Let us review the military branches of service as a viable foundation for a law enforcement career. Recognize that the armed forces exist for the sole purpose of protecting and serving the citizenry, country or interests of the United States of America. This means that all branches of service will train you to be both physically ready to defeat combatants as well as making you mentally ready to utilize all weapons and systems available. Do you see the direct and unmistakable correlation to law enforcement yet?

Extensive Job Choices

The core mission in the military branches will always be defense of the nation. So in pondering military enlistment, consider that the military is a self-sufficient world within itself. There are many non-combat military jobs that are available supporting the mission.

This means you will enjoy extensive job choices based on either mission-oriented careers or careers in support of the mission. The Navy and Army are the largest branches of service and therefore, they offer the most choices for job diversity. Again, everything from musicians to dental hygienists are employed in military service. The Marines, Air Force, and Coast Guard tend to offer more mission specialized positions. Which one is best for you obviously boils down to individual decision-making choices, compounded with what you are eligible for based on your test scores.

The job vacancies that need filled at the time of your potential enlistment is also a big factor in the equation. Your military eligibility is largely based on an approved test with the final results creating your options. Most branches offer what is commonly referred to as the ASVAB military test. This means that if you choose the military, you should take the time to prepare for this test.

Actively Prepare for Your Future

When I took my test, the military recruiter drove to my home and picked me up along with two other candidates. One of those men, a white dude from the Burns Heights housing projects in Duquesne, Pennsylvania, failed so badly that the recruiter laughed out loud all the way home and said he was not eligible for any of the jobs. I remember thinking how sad his life was and how few options there were for him. He definitely was not worldly; I doubt he was very educated. Dare I say he was likely a product of his environment? It was all about being cool and tough, not really focused on being successful. I used to be there so I can relate to him. What drove him to take the test, only he knows. I wrote this book for everyday less than average guys just like him, and well educated organized people as well—to clearly educate many on this career field to provide a segue into this satisfying career.

Problems Become Assets in Policing

I care because I really struggled in my youth. In hindsight, I was blessed with a loving family who taught me the right values. Today, our society is losing a great deal of value based initiatives. Even when you have a good family, you are still competing with the outside world. Good people are under siege in my old neighborhood. In my youth it was an embarrassment to live in the housing projects, but the decent people there were working to get ahead, improve their lives or get back on their financial feet. Today, much of the incentive to work toward a better life is gone. Now many people feel a source of pride to get over on the system and get a third-generation free ride. The term "housing projects" is outdated—those are dirty words with a negative stigma. Currently in use is the term "housing community." I got into a fight with a teen in ninth grade biology class because he made fun of me for having food stamps. It was belittling. Today many working families struggle, while scammers have full refrigerators. Most people I arrest today have way more food and much nicer stuff than I will ever have. It is indeed a strange system.

Wherever you end up, whatever your life experience and position, remember that the police and the military hold people accountable. PERSONAL RESPONSIBILITY—get some! No matter what everyone else is doing.

Minority / Female Recruitment

As previously mentioned, law enforcement agencies around the country are actively and aggressively seeking female AND minority recruits to fill positions. Many agencies initiate specific campaigns in addition to their regular recruitment efforts; designed to attract such applicants. These recruitment efforts are often ad campaigns on buses or radio ads on channels that target a focused audience. Good people of all races and genders are always encouraged to apply. In many minority communities strained relationships with the police make it extremely difficult to recruit. Persons in administrative positions must then respond to these perceptions by addressing any flaws in hiring processes, addressing public opinions of these issues, and developing corrections for any flaws in hiring practices.

To summarize: If you fall into a recruitment category, *awesome!* Maybe now is the right time to consider a job in law enforcement. Law enforcement agencies offer incredible job security in today's troubled economy, as well as rich and rewarding experiences. Again, great people are always needed who bring a fresh perspective and a healthy mind. Law enforcement needs people from all walks of life, especially persons who are grounded in honorable beliefs and strong enough mentally to do what it takes to enforce the law.

Diversity

But the specific issues that concern many community and minority community residents are complicated and should not reflect on recruitment or the relationship or *perceived relationship the police have with its citizens.* As we all know, every location is different along with the individual needs and circumstances. Although perception is to an extent reality, what I mean to say is *there is no substitute for good people of any gender or race to make a positive difference in the communities they serve.*

An example in Culture Wars, Drugs & Whitney the Patriot

Whitney Houston's performance of the Star Spangled Banner at the 2004 Super Bowl was incredible. The song moves me emotionally to my core every time I watch the replay. Her poise, presence, humility, and that enormous smile was a welcome tribute to the American Spirit. Her delivery resonated with our military and citizens everywhere. After Whitney's death, a fiery debate was publicized about flying the American flag half-staff in mourning. I saw the mother of a deceased U.S. Army Specialist on television who quoted the law, regulations, and the care of our flag; I knew immediately that legally she was right. New Jersey Governor Christie stuck by his decision to fly flags at half-staff in Houston's honor. Although I do not agree with him necessarily on the flag decision, he said it right when he addressed a place in our hearts and a need to humanize. United in our differences, we are very strong. Divided we fail, fall, and falter. (As of February 2013, Mother Cissy Houston has a book out remembering her daughter – http://www.latimes.com/features/books/jacketcopy/la-jc-whitney-houston-cissy-houston-memoir-20130128,0,2562318.story).

We live in a society that celebrates strife as breaking news. Instead, we should examine the common pitfalls and work to correct those mistakes. Whitney Houston made many human mistakes. Likely her drug use and the people she was involved with cost a storied career future and her life. Along the way she did some amazing things. Whitney Houston was a great American. She remains a testament to what can be accomplished. A roadmap has been left behind to follow for those interested in following her successful attributes. But recognize there is a culture war going on. Be a young person's bodyguard and tell them about the dangers of drugs, crime, and idleness.

Secure Employment with a Price.

In my very humble opinion and from the unwritten book of what is right, one should always seek a career path for the right reasons. In other words, do not be lured in by the money, benefits or secure employment without considering the whole picture of a job environment. Strong marketing schemes that target would be applicants are a big problem. Selling the job perks instead of a corporate mission statement or service mindset is deceptive and misleading.

Beware of the sales pitch rhetoric before making a serious decision on which career path you want to take. In other words, if you get sold on the money and benefits of a law enforcement career, you might end up unhappy months or years down the road. Oprah talks with Whitney about her darkest days: http://simply-showbiz.com/blog/archives/20605

A Good Public Servant is a Reflection of the People

Let's start out with a very basic notion: law enforcement is about assisting the public. Knowing you are a servant of the people is a great thing to keep in mind. Specialized recruitment efforts often equate to police departments that are under fire; or just attentive enough to address attempting to have a police force that is reflective of the populace it serves. Some of these efforts however, amount to political correctness battles that have little or no bearing on policing or law enforcement. In this profession, we simply handle business and do our job. As a prospective law enforcement officer, your job is to *recognize how to get there faster.* If you feel you may not yet qualify, get busy making yourself a desirable candidate.

Experience in Life Applied Evenly

Please note that just like a criminal justice degree, military service is not a requirement to qualify for a law enforcement career. Many outstanding officers *do not* have military experience. What they do have is extensive life and people experience. As I have explained, there is a direct benefit and correlation to service in the military. The benefits of service thus clearly outweigh the negatives, depending upon your military job and the wartime missions you experience.

Therefore, at the very least, you *will* become worldlier with military service; especially in a world where the United States is the melting pot of all cultures and where global terror continues to threaten to incur violence on American soil. This makes being worldly a wise and very desirable asset to bring to law enforcement.

My Worldly Experience

I am well-traveled with the United States Army, with military service in Japan, Germany, Bosnia, Hungry, France, and all over the United States. Personally I have also been to Brazil, Columbia, Mexico, and the Dominican Republic. My department thus benefits from my valuable life and people experience. I am a positive reflection on myself, my unit and my department every time I teach, testify, arrest criminals, investigate cases or just meet people.

What Do You Offer?

What assets do you bring to the table? I have used my experience as a former jail guard to obtain confessions; usually because offenders just know that I can relate to some of their experiences. Juvenile victims have also confided in me because of my empathetic skills which grew out of my own personal youth tragedies. Having been a ward of the court in my youth, I get it—

I understand. I can relate to a victim's helplessness and the criminal's hate; from my own days growing up hanging on the street corners. I am, therefore, also knowledgeable about the justice system's dysfunctional nature. I can see both sides.

What are *you* offering? Believe me; you have valuable skills, many of which are still undiscovered. Again, bear in mind these skills are not rooted in a criminal justice degree. The criminal justice program is just not good planting soil to cultivate a law enforcement career.

Take the Cook if You Need the Job Done Right

Believe it or not, an Army cook enlistment would provide you with the basic skill set to have a successful law enforcement career. Yes, it is an astounding but very plain fact. This is in sharp contrast to paying for a criminal justice degree. Personally, I would take the cook any day. Army cooks have to complete basic training, physical readiness standards, weapons qualification, fighting techniques, a background investigation and more. Now put that in your criminal justice degree and smoke it! (Check the Community Oriented Policing Services U.S. Department of Justice "Vets to Cops" brochure e051217473 June 2012 for further justification: http://www.cops. usdoj.gov/pdf/vets-to-cops/Vets2CopsBrochure.pdf).

> Key Point of this Chapter: *Choose the most cost effective method to a career path and determine what skills or resources you have. You can then turn them into assets.*

Photo Index

Serving at the G-20 with a nervous half-smile.
Although we were not supposed to be taking
pictures; my colleague recognized the irony of
"Free All Monks!"

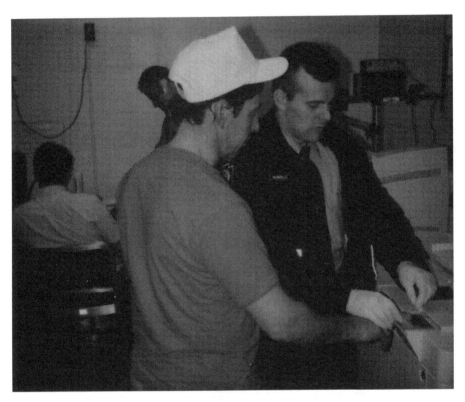

The daily routine. Fingerprinting a guy under arrest.

Leaving a homicide preliminary hearing
Reprinted with permission all rights reserved
Herald Standard Newspaper Uniontown, PA
Roberto M. Esquivel
Visual Media Editor

PART II

The Solution:

A Degree in Values

Chapter 4
MAKE AN ARREST
ON YOUR FUTURE

This is the only profession where you can save a life, take a life, or give a life.

Graduate to a New Level of Thinking.

It is time to focus on your career path. Can you follow directions? Can you interact with the public and communicate effectively in a professional way? Great! These are some of the essential ingredients to acquiring and maintaining a law enforcement career.

Remember that any venture to grow and learn is wise and noble. I absolutely applaud you for working toward any academic goals. But, please be smart. Make a focused career plan.

As I have previously stated, policing is a public service position; you move toward trouble. Any degree you acquire—not just criminal justice—will give you what can be referred to as some fundamental people exposure. This is honestly all you ever need for law enforcement, since communication with all kinds of people is vital to successful public interaction.

So, complete the tasks that will increase your chance of securing meaningful employment. Improve the odds of landing a great job; work the angles to your advantage by saving money. Diversify with a different declared degree major, which can maximize your talent, skill, and brain power.

Get a Degree in Another Major and a Minor in Criminal Justice.

Look at the points made so far in this book but do not be offended. Keep an open mind. This book is not intended to belittle or disgrace anyone at all—students and instructors alike. We are discussing candidly, not only your future, but also your finances. I am working hard to convince you to spend very little so that you can save a great deal. I want you to be "on the job" to accomplish the mission. You need the right attitude to get your head in the right place.

Probable Cause

Move forward; I want you to think about mapping out a plan. As I have suggested, consider which law enforcement agency you ultimately hope to work for in a "best case scenario." Find out now if some college accreditation is required for your career choice. Now you are planning for "on the job" with the right mindset.

Once you get there, do not be one of those common "fantasy island" types; for example, showing up for basic training in pitiful physical shape. Check the department websites ahead of time directly, or check personally with a recruitment officer or a human resource staffing civilian. It is easy enough to do, and many departments are truly in need of quality applicants. I cannot tell you how many times I have watched people go through a two-year application process only to quit within the first few days because it was too hard mentally or they were not physically fit. Really? A polygraph, psychological test, physical agility, an extremely in-depth background and a sixty-some page application. And yet, they quit in droves after the first challenge. Check your mental state and life experience for suitability. Then get yourself physically ready.

Any Discipline

The majority of law enforcement agencies require a *maximum* of sixty college course credits in any discipline and that is without a degree —if in fact credits are required by that agency at all. Many of those departments or agencies will waive thirty of those credits if you are an eligible military veteran with at least two years of active duty service. Some give a waiver for related law enforcement experience. The FBI has no such waiver for credits and they still require a four year bachelor's degree; but that is in any discipline http://www.fbijobs.gov/114.asp

Elite Graduate

Remain humble and never be fooled into thinking that as a college graduate you will be considered more elite than others applying to a department. In fact, all policing agencies have a few misguided boneheads who are incapable of applying common sense and /or decision-making, regardless of whether they have obtained a degree or not. When it comes to competency and effectiveness, all agencies suffer this fate because applicants are simply a reflection of our society.

Sharpen the Ax

The FBI as an example is unique in having many of its members who do more theory than practical hands on application. Most do not start out in uniform and are not conditioned to take charge and make split-second decisions on the street. However, Abe Lincoln is rumored to have said: "Give me six hours to chop down a tree and I will spend the first four sharpening the ax." Meaning, that when it comes to intelligent thought or rational professionalism, then usually the FBI ranks high.

Maximize Credits

Many colleges as we discussed actually give you the student thirty college credits in recognition of your military service, which simply means that upon enrollment the colleges often waive your elective credits up to thirty; for your military service experience. You then, with your military documentation, apply these credits at that institution to be credited as your electives toward a degree or discipline. When you have located a desirable law enforcement department during your job search and you determine they require college credits. Meet the standard quickly by enrolling where your experience will be recognized.

Remember to at least consider that military service pays you and eases the way for a background investigation. You will have already completed a military background *and* you are halfway there with "credit" for service that can be transferred to college elective credits. This translates simply to being paid for college credits. Take the time to talk to the military recruiters and weigh your options. Most are great, but some recruiters are fast talkers, so take a friend or a parent. Talk to police recruiters. They are awesome resources who are usually available at your disposal. Then take the time to talk candidly with the college or school you are attending or hope to attend. This is part of *the big missing link*.

How to Get Your Law Enforcement Job Faster and Cheaper

For some unknown reason, droves of young people do little, if any, research before committing themselves to investing their future in an institution of higher learning. My oldest son wanted the career and understood the physical sacrifice; yet, he had no drive or interest to read a book on the subject (especially this book, since his dad wrote it). Moreover, like all teens, he knows everything. He is content to enroll in a program as if it is the institution's responsibility. From my point of view, it is probably too much work in an instant gratification society to get actively involved in your own future. I am hopeful he will learn self-responsibility and avoid suffering the financial ramifications. I love my son, and I write this book from my heart because it infuriates and disgusts me that this marketing process is robbing young people of direction, skill, gainful employment, and a proper foundation. Plus, I was one of those young fools myself. But now you know! Apply the knowledge.

Today's youth gravitates toward these fancy sounding programs, with impressive advertising and thought-provoking classes. Young students leave the classrooms all the while filled with the arrogance and smug stupidity which is derived from these auditorium think tanks that is void of the sights, smells and sounds of the real scene.

Senior Detectives and Investigators

Again, oddly enough, many of these degree curriculums should probably be geared strictly toward senior detectives or investigators. As the criminal justice discipline has grown, what has evolved has been a marketing concept to target police departments and other law enforcement entities. Many entities are particularly buying into the concept at the administrative level that a criminal justice degree should become a prerequisite for law enforcement employment.

Under-employment

For the yet to be employed such an arrogant, know-it-all attitude usually leads to cocky unemployment or serious under-employment. Once, a twenty-year old girl showed up at the police barracks to inform me and my partner that we were all wrong in our preliminary investigation. The girl was a young college student who showed up unannounced to discuss my investigation. My colleague and I entertained her out of simple curiosity and also to obtain the additional basic background information on her family (one member of which was the target of our investigation). Her college criminal justice program had provided her with FBI profiler training! She read us the riot act about how her grandfather did not in any way fit the profile for the pedophile sexual assault we were investigating. After schooling us properly with a warning to get it right, she let us get back to work.

Whew, to have that profiler knowledge! Her "pappy" confessed the very next day, verbally and in writing! And, that is the only story (without any details) that I am telling out of school. Although the arrest paperwork for her grandfather and the specific details are literally right to know, publicly available information, I am held to that higher calling and swore to an oath which prevents me from openly discussing the case. But you get the idea, right?

Profiler Training for Entry Level?

In Chapter 1, I referred to the FBI profiler training and related study concepts as part of Criminal Justice programming. The television drama *Criminal Minds* is an entertaining criminal drama show that depicts this real life concept for a select few. I hope I have convincingly made my point to caution you on the benefits of such a degree; until then or while you weigh in, let us shift the focus back onto "probable cause."

A Crime Is Being Committed

Probable cause is the police officer's standard burden of proof to make an arrest for a crime. It is the threshold for the basic elements which are needed to prove justification for the arrest. The legal dictionary loose definition of probable cause is *the highest constitutional degree of suspicion*—not to be confused with the courtroom or trial phases, such as the burden of "beyond a reasonable doubt." Probable cause does not mean that the arrestee actually committed the crime (for the purposes of this book, that arrestee is the schools' marketing the criminal justice degree), or that the "officer" (you the student) possesses enough proof to convict the suspect (in fact we do) or even that the suspect will actually go to trial. It does mean, however, that at the time of arrest (on your bank account and future earnings), a prudent, objective, reasonable person in the position of the officer (student) would, taking into account their knowledge, experience, and observations; reasonably believe that a crime has been or is being committed (also referred to as reasonable cause). This crime of theft has been committed against you from your school.

Rewarding But Not Glamorous

Furthermore, the entertainment industry has yet to glamorize corrections and probation officer jobs. Do you hear where I am coming from? New students are not enrolling and saying, "Yeah, in four years I will be able to land this corrections officer job." Yet, that is exactly where many graduates end up. Students actually do not know what is real and what is not; they just know that the *Blue Blood* drama show and the new *CSI Miami* show are cool, the men are muscular, the women sexy, so, heck yeah, that's what they want to do for a career. Therefore, although corrections and related professions are good, decent, valuable service-oriented paying careers, we do not see people aspiring toward, or even applying for, these positions first. Effective marketing has led students to falsely believe that they must instead first pay for a criminal justice or criminology degree.

Entertainment and Its Effect

Do you recognize that these television series shows and dramas are actually crafty, well written, intelligent, and carefully scripted modern day soap operas? The TNT network really does know drama, and AMC is original and has really led the pack with the *Walking Dead*, Hell on Wheels *& Breaking Bad*. I enjoy these entertaining shows; but I want you to remember that the shows are entertainment—not real life. Fools are actually buying clothing, bumper stickers and motorcycles bearing the Network FX's premiere *Sons of Anarchy* show. It is a make believe show! Incredibly, the program has contributed to a renewed nationwide surge in motorcycle gang membership. Closer to my home, the Pagan motorcycle gang is an active motorcycle club in the western Pennsylvania area. Since the show era, they no longer discreetly meet at their clubhouse. Instead, they have an enormous sign displaying the club name and logo while busily selling T-shirts. They are blatant, lawless, self-serving criminals with mostly nothing but selfish intentions. Those of us in law enforcement must stand by in frustration as gang members laugh at our honorable profession and citizens hope to buy their merchandise. Do not fret, though. Their rank and file deceive themselves and invariably learn the hard way. Jail, death, and misery most often follow. Do you remember the Hell Raisers' Ball in New York in 2002? Most of those arrested were Western Pennsylvania Pagans. http://old.post-gazette.com/headlines/20020308pagans0308p5.asp Pittsburgh Post Gazette March 8, 2002 Blast from the Past: Pagans vs. Angels.

Measure Your Own Thoughts on a Career

Let's analyze the reasons for the aggressive marketing of the criminal justice degree. Those persons who typically seek corrections and related positions understand that the positions provide decent pay and security. Such applicants do not have any illusion that the job fulfills a lifetime dream *after acquiring a criminal justice degree*. Take a moment to consider that entire concept and measure your own thoughts on obtaining a career. Unfortunately, many of the degree applicants seeking police positions are convinced that police work will be glamorous. Be sure that you comprehend that the criminal justice degree is not required, but a relevant education in your profession will—and should always—continue. In my career, I am required to qualify semi-annually at minimum with weapons, every two years with First Aid and CPR, annually with "less lethal force options," just to name a few of the requirements as well as truckloads of yearly ongoing training.

What a Criminal Justice Degree Will Get You

For the record, if you do get that degree, it is probable that you will end up in one of the following very honorable but (often lower paying than policing) positions:

- Juvenile probation (local level);
- Corrections officers (local, state, and federal departments);
- Parole officers (state and federal level).

There are other related positions; for example, loss prevention and security, but bear in mind that these positions are most often filled by criminal justice degree graduates and a mix of high school and various college graduates.

Powerful Marketing

As stated; veteran police officers and their governing bodies are beginning to take notice of the ever-growing proliferation of criminal justice degree programs. Many of the officers are enrolling in online programs. Man, marketing is so powerful!

In contrast, my former coworker, Sandy, is contemplating getting the degree. However, she has the real experience, the instructor background and the opportunity to speak and educate a class if she chooses. This is totally different to those of you who are seeking an entry level position. No matter what profession in life you choose, always remember to ask the important and meaningful questions. What do you do better than anyone else? Perhaps your skill reveals a passion and you should move in that direction. Otherwise, you might have lost an opportunity before you even start.

Accountability

Dear veteran officers and current student enrollees; Realize that the marketing campaigns for these criminal justice programs seem to suggest that the degree will assist you with a job promotion as well as add a certain amount of creditability. Really?!

Again, please check out a website that I recently stumbled across at: www.criminaljusticeusa.com which says this very thing outright. For those law enforcement veterans who are tempted or compelled to enroll, it remains important that your chosen degree has a beneficial focus on a tangible valuable benefit for your time and effort. Examples such as degrees in leadership or advanced policing issues like:

- Profiling
- Managing People
- Grant Writing
- Forensics
- Emergency Response
- Counterterrorism Training
- Minority Recruitment
- Community Policing
- Comstat
- Managing Resources
- Liability

If any of these subjects appeal to you, sign up and jump on the opportunity—but first, consider if you work for an agency that will recognize your commitment to excellence or one that will pay for these programs, and / or promote you as a result of graduation. Most absolutely will not.

Classroom over Experience

Some of these courses may not apply to you if you are an aspiring college or high school student. Even if you are a veteran officer it seems ludicrous to me that your department will acknowledge classroom learning over experience.

Of course, I fully recognize that some departments do acknowledge some of these courses, so if they benefit you in the paycheck or personally, then getting enrolled is perfectly fine and sound. No matter what, recognize that regardless of your status—whether you are an applicant seeking employment or a veteran police officer—most police departments typically do *not* reward performance. This is in contrast to the private sector, which does tend to recognize achievement and innovation.

In my hometown, near Pittsburgh, a local college is conducting an aggressive marketing campaign for a degree in leadership. The billboard ads depict young, vibrant individuals smiling next to the phrase, "I am a leader." The ads are posted on giant billboards all over the metropolitan area. I always ask loudly in my car as I pass by: *Honestly? And compared to whom?*

Leadership

Yes, I suppose if leadership means paying for classes and reviewing issues to think about, then it does have some educational exposure value. But who do you think is a greater leader? Is it the men and women with whom I serve— who have made life and death decisions in split seconds, and been exposed to countless violent assaults, suffered the gravity of stress investigating and prosecuting incredibly difficult cases—or those billboard kids?

Yet, my coworkers do not have a paper degree in leadership. Neither do battle-tested Marines, Seals, Rangers, Soldiers, Airmen, Sailors, or Coast Guardsmen. Who would you hire? I guess if I was liability based and looking for paper champions, these kids would be a viable choice. But, if I actually needed to deal with something challenging, I would tend to go with demonstrated ability. NFL Hall of Famer Floyd Little is a true gentleman and leader. Watch and listen to his 2010 acceptance speech here to see if you agree with me: http://www.nfl.com/videos/nfl-hall-of-fame/09000d5d81998a6a/ Floyd-Little-HOF-speech

The complication comes when real life hits theory. It is generally not always pretty. The challenge requires an absolute "in your face, hands on" problem-solving steeped in the kind of tension, stress, and violence that is simply incomprehensible to think tankers. Because desk jockey activities do not raise the heart rate to acceptable levels. Until these persons can show me how it is done, I will not follow them into the battlefield.

CAUTION! Real Heroes at Work

Performance is not rewarded. Performance does not matter financially or for promotion in a civil servant law enforcement profession. Bare bones minimum, you may be recognized for a case, bravery, some volunteer work, or your overall positive service. It may even lead to a promotion if you are popular with those in power; or if by chance, you are a great test taker.

Most often, it has been my experience when working with smaller agencies or local police departments that members are promoted and demoted based at times just on the mayor or chief in power. One year later, the chief may also find themselves unemployed or back on patrol. Larger agencies with big unions (Fraternal Order of Police, of which I am a proud member) tend to be immune to some of the whims of these promotions and demotions, but you will be very hard pressed to see many hard working officers rise in the ranks. Workers work, while politically motivated favorites generally get promoted. When I solve a homicide or a complicated robbery, or even instruct a meaningful class, I do not get a bump in pay or a promotion. I just get called more often to take on the next case. Union contractual issues, political favorites, and even public perception also play an enormous role in who is on top. And, who is not.

Your Name in Lights

Humbly again, I say a law enforcement officer is a civil service position, do not expect to see your name in lights or you will be disappointed.

Get Crystal Clear

Would it not be wonderful if you managed to pay for your criminal justice degree and then you started your law enforcement career at a great salary, working good shifts in a position that allowed you maximum flexibility? In theory, the answer is yes. But in the professional world, the answer is usually no.

To save time, money, and lots of stress, remember what is important and focus on realistic goal completion. Get crystal clear. Do you know anyone who graduated and is doing great? If so, then you have a mentor or role model you can follow; otherwise, please listen to me.

Intelligence Is an Education.

Do you believe that education only means going to college? If so, you may want to get a mental checkup and, more importantly, rethink your ideology at least in this profession. Ask your professors or instructors to list some of the real-world benefits or examples of what your degree will do for you upon graduation.

The police do tense work, and most bad guys cannot be dealt with utilizing the effective communication skills taught in the classroom. Dealing with high and intoxicated persons in very desperate circumstances requires a close proximity, hands-on policing approach.

This approach does not involve any college rhetoric or classroom hypothesizing. It is real time when it comes to speaking to what they (the subjects) deem important and effective at the time; or else it is a laying of the healing hands. Halleluiah! We do more conversions than all of the television preachers combined! As human beings, each of us receives a wide and elaborate series of various educational opportunities every day, most of which are understood, rarely discussed, and ultimately, the basis of essential and meaningful life conditioning. As a matter of fact, the value you place on your own individual life experiences will ultimately shape your future, for better or worse.

Be Smart with Your Time and Money

So to date, no criminal justice degree is required for the law enforcement profession—just good common sense (a dying trait). Paul Harvey, the renowned radio announcer and storyteller, had a tag line that emphasizes the point, "And now, for the rest of the story." Position yourself for success and achievement. The time and energy spent on a criminal justice degree is a crime – for entry level. Harvey's legacy is available at: http://en.wikipedia.org/wiki/Paul_Harvey

Act 120 (PA) and Similar Accredited Schools or Police Academies

Do you want a solid tangible return on your investment? If you are not hired directly, but aspiring to get program accreditations that will get you employed faster, then consider the following example. This example from Pennsylvania may apply to all states under a different legislative title or guideline. To walk you through what needs to happen, please follow along. If an individual who was not employed by a police department wanted to become an eligible police candidate, he or she could enroll in a police academy or accredited college or university to obtain certification (as differentiated from a degree). The Pennsylvania Municipal Police Officers' Education Training Commission sanctioned training (referred to as "Act 120") would cost about $5,000, depending on the school. That is significantly less than $70,000 for a criminal justice degree! Find out what your individual state requirement is as soon as possible to determine if it is even an option, especially if such an option piques your interest.

Focus on Results and a Plan.

So, to be certain that you are following my suggestions, let me say it another way. Each state or municipality has a different set of governing rules for determining the process to become a sworn law enforcement officer. The federal government also has a set of rules, policies, and processes to become a sworn federal officer. Regardless of what rules govern you, understand that none of them recognize your criminal justice degree as a precursor to law enforcement approval. The degree means nothing more than college credits or a diploma if those credits are job stipulations.

Police Basic Training Academy

You still must pass a background investigation and go through a lengthy, and very challenging, police academy program. In West Virginia, the state police still conduct all police basic training. In Pennsylvania, the state police originally conducted all basic training. However, since the late 1970s, several universities and colleges as well as local policing agencies now conduct, "Approved Act 120," or similar "Basic Training." Act 120 is the legislative bill that was ultimately submitted to the state legislatures and approved.

Do not Get Buried in Debt

Simplified: there are thousands of people in Pennsylvania paying thousands of dollars and getting buried in debt to obtain a criminal justice degree. Most will not become police officers but may work in a related law enforcement field. Meanwhile, the vast majority who have paid for the Act 120 Police Academy accreditation Basic Training Program will, more often than not, obtain police employment in and outside of Pennsylvania because they are now *specifically qualified*. Even those people will very often struggle working for several years part time (in Pennsylvania) until gaining full-time employment with a department or agency. I have seen many West Virginia State Troopers leave policing to become Pennsylvania Corrections Officers just because of the salary and benefits.

Just Not Smart

Meanwhile thousands will parade into college and pledge thousands of unearned dollars to a bunch of professors who theorize "the job." At the very, very best you will be taught by retired adjunct professors, including some "do nothings," braggarts, and command staff administrators. Writer and Military Veteran Jack Kelly who writes for the Pittsburgh Post Gazette, and other papers, addressed this with his twice published article, "The Costly College Scam." Given that police work is your preferred career choice, determine the most important considerations you have given to your desired profession. http://www.post-gazette.com/stories/opinion/jack-kelly/the-costly-college-scam-279277/

Do you, for example, hope to work in the inner city for a metropolitan department or in a suburban setting? Are your interests focused on traffic details and first responder uniform patrol type duties? Generally, this patrol option is where most of us start—sometimes referred to as the "backbone" of the profession. Is your life experience and your place of comfort out in the open, best suited for rural policing in farming areas or communities? Most states have park rangers and sheriff's departments that meet these desires.

The highway patrol or motor carrier enforcement functions often cover a wide range of state police agencies and sheriff's departments that typically extend over America's expansive interstates.

What about airport policing to enhance homeland security or carrying out these guard type functions? Jobs in criminal investigations and drug interdiction are in demand everywhere, with little or no chance of diminishing. The "War on Drugs" is fast-paced and violent. There are also opportunities available in probation and parole, supervising offenders or juveniles.

All of these unique career opportunities are demanding, challenging, and often times consuming, with the absolute mandate of people skills, strength, persistence, and a degree of patience to get it done correctly. This means you will make lots of mistakes; otherwise, you are not human. Are you ready? Not so fast.

Special Skills

Who do you see yourself emulating? What special skills or traits do you have or hope to acquire? The Federal Bureau of Investigation is eagerly recruiting applicants for skilled professionals such as linguists, accountants, and statisticians, for example. Most of the people who choose to pursue the degree in the criminal justice career field as a college major actually end up as persons who are *not* qualified to take the job upon graduation. The bulk of departments that are hurting for qualified applicants and eager to recruit are *not* seeking you. Wow! Is that an expensive slap in the face! Well, at least your school built that cool new stadium.

Too Busy to Listen?

How odd this whole process is to me, and at this point it might seem odd to you. Most thinkers in my profession are too busy working to be concerned. Furthermore, we are civil servants and therefore not permitted to rant and rave like the rest of the public about the injustice. But trust me . . . if you are enrolled, it is unjust.

Take Charge People

I have often wondered why any man or woman would want to hold a position that yields such life and death power in the fraction of a second. Police officers (the real ones) are "take-charge people," sometimes humble and mentally drained in downtime. They also can be, and often are, controlling, even overbearing, both on and off the job. Their families make great sacrifices and pay a heavy toll! Nonetheless, most police officers are outstanding grateful human beings. I grew into this career choice while seeking secure employment to avoid the pitfalls of my youth and a repeat of my father's financial demise. I did not arrive with an eagerness to have power over others' lives.

Basic Training is an experience all recruits must pass through. The Major in charge of my training would frequently announce, "This is the only profession where you can save a life, take a life, or give a life." (This is a quote stated by PSP Retired Major William Reagan frequently in my Police Academy training. I understand he led the charge in the 1989 Camp Hill Riot to retake the prison http://en.wikipedia.org/wiki/State_Correctional_Institution_%E2%80%93_Camp_Hill). Truer words have rarely been spoken.

Since then, I have personally witnessed the gravity of real life, graduating to a deadly understanding.

You see, once again, this profession is not about you, nor will it ever be. Law enforcement will always remain a service position. You serve the public at large for the greater good under the auspices of "Protect and Serve." Think about it in this very common sense way, who was the baddest, tough guy gangster, hard-ass trouble maker you ever saw, met or encountered on the street or in school? Remember him? That is who you will be fighting in the street when you are on duty. And, you can expect to meet hundreds more like him.

Do Not Be Naïve.

One day, a cadet utterly amazed me when he proudly announced during a basic cadet class that he was going to use his four-year degree in forensics to begin a career in our department's Forensic Services Unit. The truth is it never dawned on him that our department is a government model of inefficiency, which is not designed to place applicants where they can best serve. The hiring process extensively covers written testing, physical ability, and background screening that literally exceeds a minimum one-year time frame. Despite the fact that the young man had plenty of time to learn about what to expect and where he would be going upon graduation, he arrived at the department's doorstep naïve and clueless. Filled with false hope, he lined himself up mentally with a bright future with the forensics unit to fall back on. Boy, did I have the heartiest of laughs! Union contracts and binding arbitration ensure that everyone is treated the same way at entry level. I told the young man, "No, you actually are not going to work in the forensics unit. Welcome to patrol duty!" He can expect to serve in patrol for three years minimum. It was clear that either the young man was not provided essential details from the recruiter or he simply failed to listen. Yet, he does have a valuable marketable degree and potentially a goal to work on. And as fate would have it, as of 2012, he made it into a position in the Crime Lab where his forensic degree is an asset with his position title now. It took him about four years to get there.

"Hollywood Factor"

To be sure, the world of television and movies are a real bear! I am certain that the cadet was another victim of "the Hollywood factor," as it is commonly referred to in my profession. Hollywood really does sneak up on everyone, even the veteran officers and supervisors who know better. No one is immune because the exposure is just too strong.

Technology Has a Powerful Influence

Today, you almost do not count if you are without the Internet, cable television, and a cell phone. Meanwhile, people in countries like Haiti and Japan continue to struggle just to survive after horrible earthquakes. Here in the United States, we are validated by technology so we can stay in touch. Companies relentlessly bombard us with images, messages, and crafty sales pitches to market their products to the unsuspecting minds.

The Mansion Has Been Violated.

Napoleon Hill defined *self-control* in his book *The Laws of Success* with a stipulation, " Do not let anyone, any writing, any program enter the mansion of your mind and plant seeds of dominating thoughts until they have been permitted to be entered, analyzed, processed and tested for accuracy." How profound. I have some very bad news, though. The mansion has been violated; it happens daily to each of us, and the mind is more like a beat up, old frame house instead of a fortress of solitude. Like an invisible assailant, technology is assaulting us with carefully- crafted powerful images and messages. The messages are deeply embedded into the subconscious where they shape our attitudes. Hill's family runs a foundation in his honor here: http://www.naphill.org

Influence

Corporate media—particularly online marketing—is playing a huge role in influencing the behavior of our children. With easy access to all kinds of information, we can find lyrics to songs, quotes from movies, dance moves, or fight scenes—all at the click of a mouse. But, even more fascinating, is the sad fact that many in our culture cannot count change, speak another language or fix anything. Of course, it is difficult to compete with a blockbuster movie with visual and sound effects that stimulate multiple senses. But, bear in mind that movies do not, and cannot, influence or impede government liability standards. Thus, whatever you have seen through innovation is not always the way it is.

Admit You Don't Know Everything (Jack)

If you think you know police work from what you have witnessed on television programs and movies, then you really are in big trouble. I often hear citizens—particularly victims of property crimes—make reference to television programs, claiming to know exactly what and how police resources should be distributed. I, on the other hand, do not profess to know a lawyer's job, the plumbing trade, estimating the cost of roofing repairs. Yet, I am enlightened to hear burglary victims for example, explain to me just where to sprinkle the fingerprint dust, how to allot manpower resources to prevent this sort of thing, and how investigative options could apprehend the perpetrators. Then, they add when, and how, they would like these resources to be utilized. I guess I did not get the memo.

I am not suggesting that these well-meaning citizens do not have valid experiences or ideas and input. I am, however, suggesting that it does not make sense for those of us in real-life law enforcement to factor in the irrelevance of a scripted television episode as police work. So, realize today, that with technology and a cool song I can make an officer's self-defense or use of force ugly and wrong or I can make a shootout or murder scene into a super cool video.

Your chosen profession is not music in the making or an acceptable thrilling masterpiece. Instead, it is more often a world of despicable acts of violence, simple cowardice—a reflection of the declining values present in a civilized society. If this is your cool thrill ride, you may want to go play in an amusement park. Such a fantasy mindset will not help carry you through a twenty-five year career. You must take a cold, objective look at the influence of technology in shaping your mindset when considering a career in law enforcement.

Resources and Manpower

As a young law enforcement recruit, you likely want to secure employment and provide for your loving family. The guy hopped up on drugs who will be shooting at you may have just got done playing Play Station's "Grand Theft Auto III San Andreas." This means you are no longer a person—but the good news is that you *are* worth a high score and street credibility. Believing you will have an endless supply of resources, manpower, and adequate back-up officers at your disposal is naïve and foolish. In truth, we have become the Band-Aid on a waterfall—a cut and paste operation with a smoke and mirrors deployment, followed by great rhetoric. Unless the case is so egregious that it infuriates the politicians and the public at large, you are for the most part largely on your own. Most often that is a team of one; at least for the first couple of minutes.

Mending Broken Fences

For the sake of your future and to avoid frustration, here goes; just so you know, - crimes are not solved in an hour as depicted, for example, on *Law and Order*. Rarely will you get unlimited manpower to help solve an individual case. Most importantly, the job is not designed for you to be the star and focus of attention. And to go a step further, although we (police officers) make a huge difference overall, it is also cheaper for us to die. Because the wrongful death civil rights lawsuit is much too expensive. What I specifically mean is that when the police are forced to utilize deadly force on a criminal it is still a homicide. Legally it should be a justifiable homicide with no criminal charges filed. Regardless of arrests, we are still sued in court in a civil lawsuit for a violation of the persons Federal Civil Rights; and we pay. Therefore, if you get anything out of this book (and you should have thus far alone), please know that every tough guy gangster who has been in an out of prison, lifting weights and fighting in the street, all their life conducting illegal activities; running with guns and shooting at people, has absolutely no problem attacking you. None at all, in fact. The guy in the criminal enterprise business will jack you up to get away to stay free when push comes to shove. It is his means of survival, which pretty much comes with the territory. For the most part, the police arrest the same people over and over again. So much for rehabilitation. Though for some it does work and overall we should never give up on people. An excellent example of this is Advocate Glenn Martin of the The Fortune Society of New York City; www.fortunesociety.org. As a convicted felon for robbery, he is a strong advocate for hope; addressing the real world issues of 700,000 convicted criminals returning to neighborhoods in the United States every single year. Martin was a featured speaker for the U.S. Department of Justice Community Oriented Policing Services August 2012 Maryland Annual Conference that I also presented at (in one of the smaller side rooms!). Though, for some, it just does not work; likely because the stigma is so great and old habits die hard. We cannot just throw people away. (Hence your people skills, life experience and passions are greatly needed assets in law enforcement. This is that human connection. The constant reminder that you stand for something and your legacy changes lives).

"B.S." in Criminal Justice

Yet, most criminals were probably not on the high school debate team. Hence, the crime in theory is often the theory of "B.S." If they were on the debate team, they are likely politicians now (Just kidding, of course). But, your talk in highly stressful confrontational situations is falling on deaf ears with violent offenders. This also, is not ever included in your Criminal Justice curriculum. At the police academy, physical preparation and tactics are taught to prepare for the confrontations that are about to come your way. Remember, we put handcuffs on people who do not want to be arrested, and they often do not go willingly. Unfortunately, physical confrontation is a daily police occurrence and an absolute reality. It is never a case of, "if," but a matter of, "when," that next altercation will occur.

Usually, that means just when you are feeling sick or having an off-day, Murphy's Law will reign supreme, confronting you with an attacker. Criminal justice degrees never address these life or death threats. There is little time to analyze the situation in terms of criminological theory. You could, for example, explain to your attacker that being a combatant is a futile way to solve problems, reduce aggression or solve the legacy of his family problems. But such "talk" likely would not impress your adversary enough to make him pause. You will find that those precious fractions of a second would serve you much better if you utilized a weapon from your tool belt or some empty hand techniques designed to control the assailant. A knee strike to the groin, an elbow to the face are much more effective means of restraining an attacker. I know for a fact that the criminal justice professor does not make such suggestions in class; yet, it is widely available to the public on cable television's MMA (Mixed Martial Arts) sanctioned bouts as a rousingly popular sport.

Liability and Damage Control

Furthermore, and to be sure, maybe the saddest part of all; if you are a true badass like the criminal, whether a good person or not, you most likely will not be hired. All law enforcement work, especially police work, is now actually second to liability based mandates, busy work, and cautionary regulations which has become the true business we find ourselves in. Damage Control 101 should be one of the very first criminal justice classes taught in your program studies. However, political correctness will never allow that truth to surface. I hope that my candor does not remove your interest or passion. Please, do not get me wrong or misunderstand the overall message here. I am well aware that most of you will have some thought provoking engaging discussions in class. I certainly recognize the value of such outstanding concepts. But, I must assume you are paying under the pretense that, at least eventually, you will be eligible and interested in employment. Meaning, while I hold intelligent conversation in the highest regard as essential to intellectual growth, I also acknowledge in this instance the *so what* Clause!

Simply, and a little sarcastically, exemplifying the point that it does not aid you in gainful employment.

A Television Drama Farce

CSI is a one of today's most popular crime drama television series. But such investigations are not handled in the real world as is portrayed on the television screen. It is a television drama farce. If you were to go online to check your state police or county crime labs, you will not recognize any of the forensic scientists as portrayed on CSI. *It ain't happening, Captain!* It is highly unlikely that you will graduate with your degree to be hired as the lead investigator for a forensics lab or the police department. In ninty-five percent of the agencies you will start in uniform after completing the academy or an accredited school. A few "progressive" agencies do choose to put young officers undercover (like the show and recent movie 21 Jumpstreet). Other agencies, such as the Federal Drug Enforcement Administration (DEA) do conduct almost all their operations undercover.

A Curriculum without the Basics

The academic curriculum you will have to pay for fails to provide you with the basics you will need for the first few years in any police department. It is now the current trend for criminal justice schools to work closely with police departments and coroner's offices, for example, to lend credibility to their program. This allows the prospective law enforcement recruit to see the sights, hear the sounds, observe an autopsy, do some ride-alongs, and become an auxiliary or reserve officer. But, "seeing the sights," builds up the expectation that you will be wowed into thinking something amazing, interesting and meaningful is about to happen.

A Disappointing Letdown . . . The Truth Is You Are Paying to Get Duped

You might as well get in the ring with a mixed martial arts fighter. It will be just as thrilling, stimulating, challenging, and with the same quick and painful twisting of your guts . . . but less expensive. When you are lying flat on your back on the hard canvas, staring at the knockout stars dancing in your head and feeling the disappointing let down, realize what you have— probably a low paying security job. I recently instructed a local police academy class where several students told me they paid thirty dollars to observe an autopsy. I have attended about ten such autopsy events in my career. Yet most police officers have never attended autopsies but are still receiving their paycheck. While I admit there could be some valuable evidentiary knowledge to be gained, witnessing an autopsy is like bungee jumping—cool to say you did it but not good for much else, especially at entry level.

Can We Say "Meaning"?

Do you really want a good paying job that is demanding, dangerous, complicated, and rewarding? One where you start at the bottom doing lots of "dirty work?" If so, maybe you are on the right path and have found your purpose, which is or may be a chance to serve.

I invite you to double check the facts presented in this book. I can assure you that my facts and research are solid and based on reputable sources; there is no guessing or theorizing about anything. A Google search of "Criminal Justice" yielded the following results. (Recognizing that new ones are added and deleted daily):

- Phoenix.edu
- Criminal Justice Classes USA.com
- www.ITT-Tech.edu/Criminal Justice
- criminology.fsu.edu
- Nat'l Criminal Justice Reference
- Serv: ncjrs.gov
- Choose Devry.com
- Criminal Justice Schools.com
- Collegebound.net/Crim Justice
- Criminal Justice.EarnmyDegree.com

- Online.Westbound.edu/Criminal Justice
- Mountainstate.edu
- Myonlinecriminaljusticedegree.com
- Guidetoonlineschools.com/criminaljustice.html
- Academicinfo.net
- Umuc.edu/Criminal Justice

The Google search, "Criminal Justice Degree Funding" yielded the following results:

- Allcriminaljusticeschools.com/criminal justice-financial aid
- Ehow.com – continuing ed (cites Dept. Homeland Security Scholarship)
- Directdegree.com –Twenty-nine percent increase in demand stemming from Sept. 11th

But the actual real job requirements can be found on police department recruitment websites:

- The New York City Police Department (under requirements) requires an NYPD Exam and *any* sixty college credits. http://www.nypdrecruit.com/academy-prep/hiring-process
- The Los Angeles Police Department (under requirements) requires a high school Diploma. http://www.joinlapd.com/qualifications.html
- The Pennsylvania State Police (under requirements) stipulates *any* sixty college credits with thirty credits waived for two years or more concurrent active duty service in any branch of the military or two years full time with any Police Department as a member in good standing. http://www.patrooper.com
- New York State Police: www.nytrooper.com\qualifications.cfm: any sixty college credits; thirty waived for military; no felonies.
- California Highway Patrol: www.chp.ca.gov\recruiting: age 20-35, high school diploma; prefers college degrees in English and Math.

- Baltimore City Police: www.baltimorepolice.org: tests frequently and has excellent recruitment marketing videos.
- New Orleans Police Department: www.nola.gov: Check their "Before you Apply Form," as with all these sites. The site reinforces all that I told you because it's the truth! The above named sites are just a few of a much longer list. Any department that interests you can generally be searched extensively online. Go check my facts and quit getting duped by marketing hype.

Extremely Poor Use of Your Options

For the last time, I am not suggesting that a criminal justice degree is totally worthless or without any merit. I *am* saying, however, that the time and money invested in such a degree is an extremely poor use of your options and financial resources. The key points I am making herein will help equip you to successfully secure future employment. With this in mind, this book is rooted in a deep commitment to true service, with only your best interests in mind and from an agency perspective ensuring the recruitment of the best applicants in this field. Is that someone you? Only you know. What do you value? The 2011 Christian Police movie "Courageous" outlined a strong basis for faith in God. In the process the movie lays out acceptable values and absolutely honors the profession. It is a great movie that highlights not only this profession, but also great men of character. http://www.courageousthemovie.com/themovie

Sworn to Tell the Truth

Once again, I mean absolutely no disrespect to academicians out there who prefer to theorize the ideals of our nation's Constitution and people's rights. Neither do I mean to offend those who have wowed you with the scientific aspects of investigations and solvability; nor my brothers and sisters who have served and retired or did nothing and retired (because unfortunately there are plenty of those). I definitely do not begrudge any of law enforcement's retirees or current professionals for sharing their personal experiences and war stories and bringing those realities or third-hand renditions to the classroom. With that said, in our profession, we are sworn to tell the truth. So, find some value in something I am possibly overlooking; petition the legislatures to mandate the college criminal justice degree as a job requirement or accept the cold truth that it is largely a B.S. (Bull Shit) degree! I learned what I needed to learn from a criminal justice degree in my ninth, tenth, and eleventh grade civics classes, "we hold these truths to be self-evident..."

Key Point of this Chapter: *Set your course for your career plan.*

Chapter 5

IDENTIFY THE SUSPECT
HOLDING YOU BACK

A society that demonizes the police better learn how to make friends with its criminals.

As seen posted on a wall at the barracks in the weight room in early 2001.

You Are an Asset

I suspect that professors and adjunct professors across the country are going to be furious with me for telling the truth. Many may argue semantics or digress with intellectual rants. In the meantime, without being disrespectful, take the challenge by asking your professor a few direct questions, "How many felony arrests have you made? How many serial killers or serial rapists have you profiled? What is your experience to teach this material?"

You Are Being Deceived

In fairness to the professors, I doubt that many, if any, of your instructors would have a number of arrests—that is, if they have done any field work. I personally could not respond with a hard number, but it is a bigger number, rest assured. However, that is not the point. One should be prepared for a hostile response from them, which is why I really do not advocate the questioning or challenging of them much at all. Simply because it will offend the inexperienced professors and those arrogant types who unfortunately see it as challenging their authority or position.

As a firm believer in making personal assets the most marketable product, I encourage you to have your personal affairs in order (not always easily done – just ask me!) and then obtain employment instead of paying for it first. Planning is an essential ingredient of a successful life, but as I have pointed out several times; these college degrees are not the essential. So when choosing one or the other, choose enrolling in the Sworn Officer Certification Programs; if one exists in your state. Use the shortest medium. Five thousand dollars instead of $70,000 wins every time in my checkbook or loan repayment plan. What about your budget and financial assets? Consider the military.

A New Entity – Homeland Security

On July 24, 2010, I watched a news report, "Breaking Story." The investigative reporter stated that she "uncovered" over 2,000 companies and 13,000 government agencies (local, state, federal) actively engaged in the intelligence business, with most located in and around Washington D.C. According to this reporter. I am certain that statement is true, since the proliferation of intelligence agencies was a direct result of the 9/11 attack on our country. She advised the Department of Homeland Security is building the largest government building in the country. Do you think for one minute that any local, state, or federal government agency, let alone police department, is begging to hire you based on your knowledge of the criminal justice system? The answer is, "No." Our country was attacked in a despicable manner where thousands were murdered in New York City, Washington, D.C., and Shanksville, Pennsylvania. But, do you suppose that after you study the United States Constitution and correctional rehabilitation all will be well and that your classroom learning will somehow help us to combat the new terrorist threat? In this world, law enforcement places you squarely in the face of the evil forces at work. So, once again, you will become a uniformed first responder in most realms.

Valuable Marketable Skills

Can you speak a foreign language, especially an Arabic dialect? Or Spanish, which is so prevalent in most of our major metropolitan cities? If so, you may have a valuable marketable skill. Do you have exceptional computer abilities to assist with investigating online criminal activity, money laundering, or child pornography? Are you a scientist, a forensic accountant, a medical doctor, or anyone with applicable skills necessary for law enforcement in our complex society? Are you transferring, or leaving, the military with special skills? Did you serve as a Navy SEAL or work as a communications officer? And don't forget an even bigger skill—can you follow orders? Do you get the picture yet?

Dreams of Stardom

In dreams of stardom, one does not usually wish to be a stagehand, even if that is where they happily end up. Do not shoot for the bottom of the barrel with a criminal justice degree. Law Enforcement needs your skills. What are you good at? Can you blend in and work with anyone? Great! Then maybe undercover work is your thing. Identify your assets and set some goals for your path. Grow, learn and, most importantly, identify the suspect that is holding you back.

Inspiration

Dick Wolf is the Emmy award winning creator and producer of a number of popular television crime dramas. I don't know his sources of inspiration or who he employed as his program advisors. I am just a fan who truly enjoys *Law and Order* and the '80s hit show *Hill Street Blues*. Dick Wolf was not a police officer, as far as I know, and oddly enough he did not need a criminal justice degree to be so successful. He is just an Emmy award winner with a degree in passion and creativity.

Revisiting Marketing

As previously stated, I was originally inspired to write this book when, out of frustration, I began to document everything and anything job related. The writing served as an outlet to deal with many of the job hurdles I faced. I wanted to focus on solutions instead of getting bogged down in chronic venting and complaining. Look very closely at a lot of the online Criminal

Justice programs. What you should see and will now notice on many online or paper advertisements is a sufficient number of disclaimers in small print at the bottom of the add or hidden on a web page or pamphlet page buried behind a tiny asterisk. Go check and think of these asterisk hidden disclaimers as b.s. indicators; because that is what they are. One of my favorite actual advertisements is: "*Additional academy training may be required for law enforcement positions."

The advertisement should read as a translation: "Dear dumbass, if you are not sure what to do with your life, please consider being impressed with this muscle bound guy we have placed in uniform to depict a real police officer. You will note that he seems happy and appears to be handcuffing a bad person. Meaning, he is doing good helping out, plus his emergency lights are flashing. All you have to do is come in, we will actually help you fill out all forms and paperwork so the state can provide us with thousands of dollars to be paid back by you for years to come. In return, though you are not working, we will give you a small percentage to buy our books and eat our cafeteria style lunches. How does that sound? No, we don't have job placement, but many other programs do."

Despite the fact that if they do offer placement it is often in the form of security work that you could have obtained on your own. It works out for the school and the security company. The school covers themselves and actually gets you a job and the security company upgrades a little bit from their normal applicant pool. The only one coming up short is you with an under paying job and student loans overdue.

Still thousands are being bamboozled monthly under these two headings:

a. Departments are hiring; plus you know crime is getting worse.
b. *Join the Fight!*

As far as whether Criminal Justice Programs will survive and ever evolve into something of substance is well beyond my knowledge base, or even opinion. I am not sure if I have a preference either way. Maybe if the degree evolved into truly making a difference by adding value for law enforcement, especially the police which would result in benefits for citizens. (An example of this might be: www.policeandfirepublishing.com which appears to be a group of professionals who have embraced the criminal justice studies and applied their expertise in hopes of adding value to the curriculums). As of now, the overall degree still does not add the overall value. Universities that are springing up online everywhere have graduated into *huge marketing campaigners designed for profit, not for content, service and higher learning.*

Can You Rise Above and Beyond When Called?

Do not get me wrong; we have many officers who do awesome work and many more who rise way above and beyond when called upon. In the end, though, many of the new recruits end up as officers who are not adequately focused on doing a good job or giving 110 percent. Quite frankly, I cannot blame any of them. Some of these problems are generational while others are indoctrination into an overburdened system. Plus, to survive mentally and physically in a profession with so many adrenaline spikes, followed by hours of mindless accountability garbage, is an amazing challenge. And, those work environment examples do not address the endless streams of liability paperwork.

Real Police Work

Today's paperwork prevents most "real" police work, including serving the public and protecting citizens from violent criminals- from actually being done. Paperwork that makes policing even more reactive, instead of proactive, and definitely segregated from many of the communities that we serve. Does this sound much like what you envisioned? Too often, we find ourselves off the road and off the street at some liability training or typing streams of mandated documents. In the meantime, those current recruitment practices that focus strictly on the selling benefits of the career, like good health insurance, secure pay and holidays also have applicants expecting excitement. What about the mission and service at hand which should be serving the community? Guys like retired police officer, author, actor and speaker: the 1970's Newark Police Hero David Toma should be honored, recognized and consulted. (*An amazing book* to read: *Toma: The Compassionate Cop*). His success at arresting criminals was literally second only to his compassion. The book in chapters one thru four drives this fact home. I have read it personally three times. http://www.davidtoma.com. Only a fool would ignore his personal experience and wisdom. According to his website, he has a new book coming out soon entitled: *Unforgettable - The Life and Legend of David Toma*.

The World of Academia

About ten years ago, under the pretense of improving the professionalism of police work; scholars, politicians and activists really started to pound away on the police officer. With the help of news coverage, they campaigned against law enforcement, focusing primarily on the actions of police. Rest assured, I concur wholeheartedly that as a government entity any police department has the potential to become a model of inefficiency. So, while I recognize that law enforcement, especially the police, should be well trained, continually challenged, and striving for excellence, I also acknowledge that a college educated, well-read officer or a life-experienced officer is likewise desirable. It is vital to remember that personal healthy growth is the key to a large part of your awareness, suitability and success in life and police work; and that can happen, but not just because you have academic credentials.

College Credits Do Not Stop Crime or Prevent Bad Officers

When holding the police to an acceptable high standard, the public should be reminded and always remember that the police are not the cause of violence, crime, or a lack of accountability. Once you get the job, *do not* allow yourself to be demonized in law enforcement. One of my coworkers posted a sign that said, "A society that demonizes the police better learn how to make friends with its criminals." As police officers, we are the last resort response to any out of control circumstance, but not the answer; only the temporary solution. The police rule by force. That is why we have all those tools and force options on our duty belts. Police interaction is forced change and hardly designed as a democratic approach or response.

Citizens have the recourse of the courtroom when dealing with the police officer. However, American society has at least groomed our citizenry to think policing is something debatably democratic that goes down in the street. According to case law; under the authority and auspices of civil rights, citizens may now legally tell the police in public, "Fuck you," and share that heartwarming middle finger salute. How far should such hostility go— on the escalating scale of disrespect and violence toward police and the average fellow citizens? I can only hope that those persons with the ideals of placing liberal views over people's lives and circumstances should soon get the chance to meet a violent criminal.

I have heard it said that a liberal is someone who has never been mugged. Recognizing that we are the sum total of experiences, I am a fair "turn the other cheek" guy. Yet, I once was told when my co-worker's sister was robbed at gunpoint and later the victim of a car break-in, her worldly innocence and liberal attitude toward punishment forever changed. I personally just realize that some people do not respond to verbal direction while others are simply passive idealists.

Liability-Based Training

The police place the out-of-control back into a manageable situation and, as such, perform the irrefutable role of policing. Through protests and lawsuits, the American Civil Liberties Union (ACLU), activists, academics, politicians, and the like to a degree, have reshaped law enforcement to an extent by requiring extensive liability training for most departments and influencing the implementation of college credit requirements for many others. In November 2011, the mayor of Los Angeles, a former ACLU activist himself, was put in a unique position. On the political talk show with host Charlie Rose, the mayor discussed and defended his decision to order the removal of protestors known as "Occupiers" from the city. In the interview, Mayor Villaraigosa was forced to defend the police actions of physical removal, arrest, and violence at his direction as "necessary."

As a whole, law enforcement has accepted the standard blame and liability requirements that come with this profession. In reality, very few of these mandates actually assist you or the citizen in results or job performance. And, the same goes with the criminal justice degree. Neither liability requirements nor criminal justice degrees speak to the actions of criminals. I have consistently utilized the contrast example of a father, parent, legal guardian, teacher or other interested party providing direction as a comparable segue to policing.

In today's culture, people frown upon obedience, compliance, and respect as signs of weakness. In truth, these behaviors demonstrate strength and self-control. Yet, very few people listen because everyone wants to talk to be the center of focus. Self-centered behavior and poor listening abilities constitute some of the police officers' biggest woes and are the main reasons for escalating violent confrontations in our culture. Confronting each of us in life, and definitely in policing, are people void of accountability or remorse. This makes for a very dangerous recipe, indeed. Trouble is brewing and it is boiling over! Welcome to too much heat in your professional kitchen. Can you stand the heat?

The Higher Standard

Accruing the credit requirements for employment and receiving the additional awareness training is not necessarily a bad thing. Any venture to grow, learn and educate oneself is wise and noble. So when you become employed by any government entity, seeking additional training and certification requirements can be beneficial to the public, the officer, and ultimately, to the department. Certainly the law enforcement community should be held to that higher standard to win or maintain the public's trust and confidence. After all, our profession does hold the tremendous power to take away people's freedoms.

The Real Nagging Problem

Yet, while the police are continually being grilled and blamed, the public we serve continues to morally decline, decay and challenge any authority.

There is mutiny on the horizon. I am grateful for those knuckle draggers in our profession—those hardened, callous individuals who are often just as violent and dangerous as the criminals they strive to arrest. When this breed of officer is finally weeded out (and the system is working on it) it will be a sad, sad day for the honest, hardworking citizens of this country.

Passivity— Do NOT Pass It On!

Good people are in danger of becoming lambs for the slaughter, and many of this *only* college educated generation of officer, lacking practical life and people experience, have been groomed into passivity to their own detriment and demise.

I implore you to take a few moments to read the story of Dr. William Petit and what criminals did to him, his wife, and daughters during a home invasion on July 23, 2007 in Cheshire, Connecticut. (www.topics. nytimes.com/top/reference/timestopics/.../p/petit.../index.html). Though he was severely beaten, Dr. Petit survived the attack. But his wife and two young daughters were raped, murdered, and burned to death in their own home. He is a good Christian man whose faith has been rocked to its core. (Reference Oprah Winfrey interview). No person should ever have to endure such a horror. I am also a good Christian with again as much turn-the-other cheek compassion as a human guy can stomach. But most criminals simply are not; too many are high on drugs and out of their minds making them therefore incapable of rational thought. Most of these individuals are also selfish, valueless, violent people. So, if you are coming aboard the ship of law enforcement, you better be like *Billy Jack* ('70s tough guy), *Shaft* ('70s police officer), Steven Segal ('90s martial arts Aikido tough guy). A hands-on member prepared for action.

RECAPPING – DEBUNKING OPERATION PRETEND

Again, the degree (depending upon school) is generally a breakdown of crime, punishment, and rehabilitation in the United States. Often times, they woo you with the forensic science exposure. It *appears neat and super important.* That is not what a criminal justice degree will help you to do— for entry level. Get a forensic science degree instead, if science piques your interest. Get a psychology degree; it will serve you better dealing with people and the many problems they face. The F.B.I., again as a truly excellent example, heavily recruits accountants, linguists, medical professionals—not criminal justice majors—but they will take you – only if you can pass an extensive background, though

Hence, it is largely *a meaningless degree*. Unfortunately, many probation officers, juvenile detention and juvenile group home workers already have these degrees and get paid very little or generally, just less. Spend your money, your parent's money, or your military G. I. Bill wisely. Become a law enforcement officer in any profession without spending more than the money for this book. The facts are clearly explained and in the upcoming pages we will discuss what should be your focus -in depth.

Key point of this chapter: *There are too many broke, angry and disappointed Criminal Justice majors out there.*

Chapter 6

CREDIT, HONOR AND FITNESS

The only thing you have and take with you in this life is your reputation. You have a lifetime to build it, but it can be ruined in seconds. Guard and defend it.

What is Really Required? Can you be Superman with a Clark Kent Lifestyle?

By now, there are only two relevant questions to answer when planning a law enforcement career:

1. Do you possess the necessary decency in morals, mental capacity, and appropriate value system to do the job up to the legal standard?
2. Are you physically capable of meeting the minimum qualification entrance requirements?

Once you comprehend these straightforward and relatively simple thresholds, it becomes imperative that you know that they are the very essential basic two levels of acceptability. Political correctness and liability have added other standards.

Never Beat Yourself Up

In examining the additions to these standards, recognize that most of us have fallen a prey to effective marketing. Do not beat yourself up. Just move forward now that you have become educated and focused. Check the U.S.

Department of Justice COPS Office "Innovations in Police Recruitment and Hiring" DVD, which is free FOR Law Enforcement: http://www.cops.usdoj. gov/pdf/publications/e06071391b.pdf . There is nothing included on a criminal justice degree; yet plenty on obtaining an education.

What does a Criminal Justice degree really say?

The answer is: "nothing!" I have gained a mild bit of entertainment in the form of on the job satisfaction arresting the occasional criminal justice major. They usually feel inherently confident in knowing all things law related. As an officer who has been subjected to their verbal legalese and enlightened indulging their pointless flawed rants. These "experts" enjoyed lecturing me with their versions of what I, as an officer of the law, could and could not do (according to their professor). "My Professor says . . ." is the same basic rhetoric found in Adam Sandler's movie *Waterboy* when his character Bobby tells the Colonel Sanders College professor that he is wrong and Momma is right; on the subject of the crocodile's brain. It is that kind of logic! A simple "Yes, Sir" might have served them better, but to each his / her own, right?

Graduate

Let us "graduate" to a higher level of practical (common sense) thinking. To provide a direct quote from my astute and currently retired Lieutenant Supervisor, "Under this current regime of thinking in our department, you can have an associate's degree in basket weaving and be qualified to apply." He meant that the college requirement for sixty college credits in any discipline (with or without a degree) does not really mean anything in terms of law enforcement career application! It is the knowledge, life experience, mature values and resources you bring with you that ultimately, in turn, brings honor to the profession and yourself.

Be relevant and meaningful. Diversify and create options for your future. I would almost prefer to see the basket weaving degree than what many of today's youth are choosing to take to apply to their future career.

Decent, Qualified but Unprepared

It is painful to watch the destruction of your financial future. I have personally trained a couple boat loads of criminal justice majors in basic police training; as many as eighty students in the last ten classes. Some departments, including mine, are missing out on a tremendous amount of exceptional and decent qualified applicants who were only excluded for credits, minor infractions or tedious mistakes. Many possessed worthy life experiences which would have made them phenomenal candidates.

Unfortunately, because they do not have sufficient college credits, or because they have minor blemishes in their life history, they are disqualified under the umbrella of liability from serving in law enforcement. All military veterans who do not have at least thirty college credits are also disqualified. In the land of common sense, it is simply incredible to exclude a veteran only to hire a person who has never held gainful employment because they were eligible to obtain student loans.

When political correctness turns its head, look out! So are we clear? My own department mandates recruits with college credits; (As of 12/13 my Department is waiving credits for veterans); but the credits do not have to be in a criminal justice discipline. You have been educated and are now familiar with the standards. Go forward to create options and opportunities. You will be a valuable asset. My sister gave me Brian Tracy's book *Goals* in my mid-thirties. The straightforward clarification of planning, establishing what you want and writing it down was a very eye opening, exciting, never covered in school or college concept. So be clear.

Now hear this: You do not need a criminal justice degree. I intend to help you save thousands of dollars and encourage you to move on to another discipline in the school of your choice. There you can get a meaningful degree and still obtain a law enforcement career. And that is the "rub" (street slang for irritation) for criminal justice graduates—knowing they achieved next to nothing and owe $60,000 to $70,000. Do you hear what I am saying? The Army can, and does, promote you up to an E-4 specialist rank upon entry level as recognition for college credits—without a degree as soon as you are accepted into this Branch of service. The Army rewards recruits with college credits that do not have a four-year degree with a higher rank upon entering; meaning that with a four-year bachelor's degree you enter the Army as a commissioned officer. With college credits you increase your rank and pay grade before experience at entry level. In law enforcement, however, with the criminal justice or criminology degree you get no such opportunity.

I am grateful to a recent graduate of the criminal justice discipline who shared with me a piece of wisdom garnered from his professor; namely the acronym for criminal culpability: "RINK" which stands for Recklessly, Intentionally, Negligently, Knowingly. Though this graduate's kernel of knowledge is worth thousands of dollars on any given day, he is currently a uniform patrol member. The department did not send him right to the top of the ranks for his criminal justice degree experience.

Regardless of where you apply and what degree you have in your résumé, if any, a solid and unblemished background is essential. Be prepared to be as innocent as the Virgin Mary— seriously. You will be investigated and scrutinized extensively for suitability.

Far too many of you who are enrolled in the criminal justice degree program are messing up your chances for a decent paying job with a department as a sworn law enforcement officer because you continue to drink excessively, tattoo and pierce everything on your body and basically overall just act like an average, immature American jackass. As opposed to, say, being the real leader that you had hoped to be as an officer. Music rap artist Eminem rocks the microphone as a significant music rapper. His ballad with singer Rhianna, "Love the Way You Lie," has earned him millions of dollars and star recognition. But emulating his lyrics will get you immediately disqualified or dismissed.

At the Core

If it is not too late to turn it around, I strongly suggest you get to work. This means in essence that you begin to *subscribe to certain core values and behaviors to succeed as an applicant*. Depending on the department of your choice, any criminal arrests you have sustained will potentially get you disqualified. Any arrest will be reviewed, whether committed as a careless mistake or in an oblivious stupor at spring break in Cancun, Ocean City, Wilmington, Daytona or Fort Lauderdale.

Lowering Your Chances

It is true that some departments have adapted to society's growing tolerance for what would otherwise be unacceptable behavioral norms and problems. Acceptance of certain arrests might just be to get a pool of eligible applicants as required by law. In other words, telling everyone "go ahead and apply"; while knowing that many applicants will not survive the careful scrutiny of job requirements. The now very common violations, such as driving under the influence, also called driving while intoxicated, for instance, have enormous ramifications for any policing agency or any agency that permits you to drive as part of your employment. Such a crime (i.e., driving while intoxicated) can lead to death, destruction, and civil liability.

Therefore, even though on paper you are still eligible with an exemption as a first offense for many departments; you can rest assured it is still considered a crime and that such an offense will likely muddy up your otherwise good reputation. Although every one of us does make mistakes, and it is certainly understandable that just a few drinks will get you to reach the legal limit, you personally now have yourself in a bind. The act of drinking and then driving itself is construed as basically irresponsible, incredibly expensive, and definitely a life-changing event if your actions or your driving results in harm to another person.

Liability and the Purpose of Law Enforcement

This brings me back to the entire reason for the enforcement efforts in the first place. Driving is a privilege in every state, and carelessly operating a several thousand pound vehicle has dire consequences. We function in a society that relies on the use of motor vehicles. If you get caught, it is possible that your criminal arrest record would be expunged if you pay a large fee and attend classes. However, you appear dishonest when and if discovered since media outlets and other sources also record this information through the current 'right to know' laws. If you do become a police officer, any subsequent offenses could cause your department to be liable because they were aware of your past as you have now established a pattern or history. Liability is the name of the game, which now positions you as a potential drunk. This is in sharp contrast to how much fun the movies portray drinking and driving

My department checks grades and school attendance all the way back to the tenth grade. Any blemishes, teen mistakes or the misguided actions of youth generally do not go unnoticed in the pre-polygraph interview or the polygraph test, which most often or typically spells unemployment for you. This includes your www.Facebook.com rants! Take a close look at your past. Have you made mistakes? Yes, we all have and we continue to make mistakes every day. I mess up as soon as my feet hit the floor out of bed each morning. You will be looked at with scrutiny upon the inception of employment forever because you now represent something much bigger than yourself. Police officers refer to this as living in a fish bowl, which infers that everyone is looking in at you and you need to have your head screwed on a 360° swivel to protect and defend your actions and encounters. From here on, everything you do is a reflection of the responsibilities you uphold in your position. You will never be referred to as Mr. or Ms. or Mrs. again; you will be referred to as "Officer," "Trooper," "Sergeant," etc. This is 100 percent true for corrections officers, parole officers, and the like. Again, we all fall under the police umbrella. So, the premise being that if it is this career field you seek, it really does not matter since from a law enforcement standpoint the media and public will view you in the same light. You are painted with the same brush as an "Officer" who will (and should) be held to that much higher standard. How do your neighbors and your friends perceive you? This is the relevant measuring standard for job longevity.

These are incredibly important values and standards to meet. Compare society's view to the criminal who is innocent until proven guilty. The only thing you have and take with you in this life is your reputation. You have a lifetime to build it, but it can be ruined in seconds. Guard and defend it. It is pretty much a no-brainer that your background investigator will discover some of your youthful indiscretions. I would count on it, but perhaps you might consider it only a possibility, right? I guess you could hope for an incompetent or overworked investigator. There are plenty of them. I was, in fact, a background investigator for what seemed like an eternity. I was super busy, but definitely not incompetent. Juggling sixty to one hundred major cases at a time is daunting. But chances are, you will be discovered. Are you prepared to withstand a barrage of accusatory questioning over several hours before and after a polygraph? The scrutiny could continue over the course of days, or weeks. If you don't think you can take the heat then kiss this job goodbye. Iron does actually sharpen iron. Your "metal" will be tested long before you hit the streets.

Honor

It really starts with being comfortable in your own skin, a certain maturity level. Owning your decisions, owning up to mistakes while practicing the kind of life that comes with the decisiveness that makes for an honorable person. If you do not grasp this notion, you are likely not going to make it through an extensive background investigation.

Credit Doesn't Define You, but It Might Prevent You

What about your credit score? This can play a factor, as well. Thus far, I have spelled out several key points that should have saved you a tremendous amount of time and money. Tell your friends about what you have learned from this book. I fully expect the college requirement to become a mandatory state or nationwide requirement in the future with the way schools are campaigning. The beginning of the these new trends where the federal government's Homeland Security Office is advertising civilian analyst jobs that are requiring or recommending a criminal justice degree. Analyst jobs should not be equated with police work functions. In fact, these are typically a civilian carrying out important research tasks behind the scenes and not to be confused with hands on interaction out in the field.

Broke, Angry and Disappointed

Take that look closely at online criminal justice programs. Notice those substantial number of disclaimers in small print at the bottom of the ad or hidden on a web page or pamphlet page buried behind a tiny asterisk.

Do not remain one of the thousands of unsuspecting students being bamboozled by these ads declaring that law enforcement departments are hiring or because crime is getting worse, you can "Join the fight."

If the disciplines can cause results in benefits for citizens, then that would be all the better. But as of now, they do not. Citizens want guys like me and my hard working fellow officers—Pat, Tim, Matt and Scott, Frank, F.L., Craig, Jamie, John, Jim, Ed, Jeff, to name a few awesome Troopers—because we have fire, passion, and do not give up (This is my personal shout-out to a few great policemen I know well, without any last names to protect the hardworking. There are soooo many amazing officers I have not listed. Many I have learned tremendous lessons from like Don who taught me about the hidden killer – stress!).

So, as you look around, recognize that traditional schools are beginning to dwindle, and in a tough economy people are becoming more financially strapped. Something has to give. The schools springing up online are evolving into huge marketing campaigners designed strictly for profit, not for content, service and that higher learning.(This is my second time stating this for emphasis; let it sink in).

Please Think Hard! Be Smart, Plan and Listen

Our economy is currently experiencing widespread distress. Job layoffs, overdue bills, charge-offs and housing foreclosures that are common. Tough economic times do not equate to a little bump in the road. You could be compromised. Remember, we are speaking from the perspective of background investigation credit worthiness. Law enforcement departments will, as a matter of routine, move on to the next applicant if you are in the late pay, repossession, foreclosure category. Can you say "Next"? Fix your credit issues before you apply! Secure the appropriate and reputable services that can challenge your report discrepancies or write to the credit bureau yourself. Just get it done. You will be glad that you did. It is worth every penny to save the career you are so passionately seeking. Think of it as an investment. Even financial guru Dave Ramsey recommends that you do it yourself. Or, you could be content with your graveyard shift of security work for seven dollars an hour at the construction site in the dead of winter. http://www.daveramsey.com/fpu/home/?s_kwcid=TC|6886|financial%20 peace%20university||S|p|4901617826&gclid=COyu2K_9mrUCFQqk4Aods1 4ASw

When You are Soft, You are Lost

As they say out in the street, "C'mon, dog." That means to get your butt in gear—find some motivation. I hope you see the health care benefits and respectable hourly wage that is at stake. Make it a workable reality. Do your part and get motivated. The alternative is to avoid scratching that curiosity itch and letting yourself be a do-nothing. Consider what a hardened criminal will do to beat you down and break your jaw just to avoid another arrest. Check out those local news headlines. Police officers are in a violent war. Look at your local newspaper or online police blotter.

Train Hard.

Train hard like your life depends on it . . . because it does! There is a gun at every incident. Your weak, soft ass brings it. Fitness is a lifestyle. It has been a constant struggle for me since I eat for comfort, socialization, and absolutely out of frustration. Alcohol has really become a taboo option these days. And I still remain extremely frustrated at times (mostly when I'm awake). I also do not sleep from working years of all three shifts and being called out in the middle of the night. If you are not an athlete and you have not challenged yourself physically in the past, I strongly recommend that you take part in a regular fitness program, including cardio and stretching.

Police work is incredibly physically challenging and often exhausting, fighting and running with all of the equipment will deplete you if it occurs for extended periods of time. Police work means enduring long shifts, odd start times, and sedentary hours spent at a desk or in a car. Start training right now for your health and longevity.

Have you seen the training regimen for the contestants on the "Biggest Loser"? The contestants achieve tremendous results and overcome incredible odds. http://www.biggestloser.com/why-join/compare-features?_source=Reso_BLC_Brand&hcoref=search&WT.srch=Google&sky=biggest+loser+work+out&nlcid=SEM

Multiply those results by ten as a police officer. You will have to be physically fit on your journey confronting lawlessness. The guys getting out of jail today are incredibly strong, muscular, violent and highly skilled in fighting techniques.

Your Customer Base

Do your criminal justice classes prepare you for intimidating body tattoos, thousand yard dead-eye stares, psychological intimidation, and overall physical roughness? Ninety-five percent of those "gentlemen" understand only one thing: force. You will learn that if you appear docile, indecisive and passive, criminals will assume you are weak. If you are perceived as such, you are in trouble and likely to be assaulted, disrespected, or far worse.

That is why most police officers are not the helpful fellows you were conditioned and raised up to believe they were. They are often giant jerks most times if they are worth their salt. I do not agree with disrespecting the public at the onset of interaction, but one should be able to flip on a dime to get to ugly quick for survival and a winning edge.

If I had my pick for back-up at a violent crowded bar fight, would I want Polly Polite or Slammin' Sammy, the knockout king. Yes, you guessed it. It's going to be me and Sammy, whether he has a winning personality or not. It's simple; my family would prefer if I came back home after my scheduled shift. And, when your family is at stake, you don't want a "stand around" liability-based joker for a partner or back up.

A Hero-ific Job

They call it policing. In a perfect world, you would want a polite, well-educated, and decent officer as a partner. But in the real world negativity from bad guys rubs off. Deal with it. You do not have to like us, but we do perform a hero-ific job. I could not be prouder to be associated with some of the greatest men and women this world has seen. This service job really, really can wear you down if you are not prepared and without a plan. Long term application without vacations, good family time, or relaxing hobbies can cause mental fatigue, physical burnout, cynical episodes, and lasting frowns. Prepare to stay hero-ific.

The Penny between Your Toes

Although the polygraph is not approved for courtroom proceedings, the polygraph exam is a staple in criminal investigations for cooperating suspects or fact witnesses. It is also a very common tool for background investigations for new hires, which leaves you with no stipulation or option to decline. In other words, unlike the criminals, you cannot decline unless you do not want the job.

Defeating a polygraph is at best a maybe proposition. There are several publications and Internet sites claiming to teach you how to defeat the polygraph. But if you have a pulse and a conscience; I'm confident that more often than not the polygraph will detect a deceitful or lying person. The penny between your toes won't save you. The test is no better or worse than the examiner. Baseline testing and follow-up questions are essential keys to revealing the truth. So, make your answers the truth. If you have a heartbeat and a conscience, any lies could potentially be uncovered.

Common Automatic Job Disqualifiers:

1. Admission of marijuana use within three years of the application process.
2. Multiple public intoxication arrests, multiple DUI/DWI arrests, and any abuse of prescription medication.

3. Admission of theft as an adult from employers or retailers.

4. Any and all false statements discovered during the application process and any related dishonest acts, such as cheating or omissions of pertinent information for the same reasons as the above.

5. Admission of substance abuse and/or including the selling of illegal or prescription drugs constitutes a felonious offense. Illegal substances include heroin, cocaine, steroids, crack cocaine, methamphetamine, or any prescription drugs utilized without a prescription, such as oxycontin, valium, even 800 mg ibuprofen. Disqualification also applies to the admission of sharing medication prescribed to another.

6. Any record of mental health commitments, especially non-voluntary (or court ordered), is an automatic and immediate disqualifier. This is an automatic flag for prohibiting anyone committed from carrying a firearm. These are mandated by federal and state laws. Psychologist and psychiatrist visits are confidential HIPPA protected doctor – client privilege stuff. However, mental health commitments are a real challenging gray area when it comes to becoming or maintaining a sworn police officer status. Even if you have experienced horrible tragedy or depression. Always think or consider the liability factors.

7. Any domestic violence incidents; protection from abuse orders are also automatic disqualifiers for most applicants since the bulk of these orders prevent the possession of firearms. Any allegations of racial prejudice real or perceived if documented or verified by anyone will generally automatically disqualify you as a liability as well.

8. Outstanding and significant credit default history, including outstanding debts, low scores, negative reporting (charge-offs, foreclosures, repossessions).

9. Felony convictions of family members are not automatic for disqualification. However, such convictions are construed as reflections on you and the people with whom you associate.

10. Admissions to taking a family member's prescribed medications for back pain, headache, etc.

11. Downloading music illegally raises a flag for some federal agencies and state police agencies which tend to make "a federal case" out of what society largely overlooks. Illegal downloading is considered a piracy bootlegging violation and infringement of federal or state copyright laws.

12. Arrest for paying for prostitution service is regarded as sleazy and immoral. Think good little Christian, not leather and chains. If such behaviors are discovered in a background investigation. Marv Albert can still work as a basketball announcer, but you will not be permitted to work in law enforcement.

The disqualifications cited above are viewed as violations relating to character, credibility, integrity, accountability, and your overall value system. Be thorough, complete, and focused because omissions by mistake could be viewed as an overt act to be less than truthful. As you can clearly see, law enforcement officers are held to a higher standard over and above other professionals. Police yourself now or look elsewhere for a career. The list of disqualifications is not all inclusive and definitely not to be substituted as a way to get around, disguise or beat the system. Instead, these disqualifiers and questionable behavioral acts are designed to weed out violators from honest, qualified candidates. Consider these disqualifiers as gentle reminders in case you have been spending too much time with persons in moral decay or in case you have been watching too many movies.

Key Point of this Chapter: *Recognize the actual job requirements and disqualifiers.*

Chapter 7
CHECK YOUR VALUES

Law enforcement forces responsibility.

The Only Foundation You Need: The University of Values

By the time I reached my early forties, I had amassed a lifetime of mistakes, pitfalls, pain, shortcomings and disappointments. Though this brand of "master's degree" was not attained at any college, I consider the experience a valid, mature education. Providing the reflection and research that you now need to begin to develop your plan to enter into a law enforcement career. Heck, maybe even just to have a successful life either way; so without further delay, here it is summarized:

Guard, Build and Defend Your Reputation. (As referenced in the subtitle of Chapter 6). Guard, build, and defend your reputation! That is the gist of it. You are how you are perceived. What you become known for becomes you. Integrity and honor are not created or forged in the criminal justice classroom. That should not come as a surprise; yet, as the lambs that are marketed for financial slaughter, most of us let others think for us—television, movies, the Internet, college degree marketing. One of the many farces and disclaimers is that the world of academia would have you believe that somehow a lesson in ethics will forge your iron will against corruption, negativity and immoral judgment. It is never a bad idea to discuss the threshold or even to lay out some foundational lines that should never be crossed. However in truth, your life experiences and the lessons you take from them will ultimately lend the best options or choices. Although, I know

I should never say "never," it will likely be one cold day in Hell before I would compromise my own integrity. It is not about my body build or any classes I took, but simply because I am a man with a strong belief system who stands for something. When you are not informed or when you have not taken the time to carefully review what you stand for, unfortunately then it is easy to fall for anything.

Go Out and Honestly Do the Job

It seems that everywhere you look, yet another criminal justice program is being offered. The real problem is that very few people actually want to do this kind of job. Your "customer" or "client base," as many politically correct administrators like to put it, is often a lawless segment of the public filled with desperate people who unfortunately possess little or no values—at least at the time of the crime. Law enforcement officers need leadership, strength and people skills to function effectively and survive their encounters with such members of the public—qualifications that are not attained with a criminal justice degree. University professors can help law enforcement address social issues through studies, cooperative partnerships and think tank resources. Nothing, however, can replace boots on the ground and real face to face street contacts and encounters.

Find a Role Model or Mentor

If you are already enrolled in classes, take a close look at your teachers. Do they possess what you are after? In theory professors, lawyers, and academics are people who most likely have not done what they have instructed. Ask them when was the last time (if ever) they rolled around in a dark alley with some drunken bum. On the rare occasion that they had such an experience, then you should listen to their instruction. Otherwise, their instruction leaves out the only legitimate and essential ingredient that matters: real police work. For example, a heroin junkie is attacking me. I really do not care about his rights at that moment, the Fourth Amendment, his abusive childhood, or the history of crime and punishment in the United States. I just want him off of me. Period.

To take a page from Malcolm X before he went to Mecca; my goal in such a moment of confrontation is *control*, and so I justify the use of force by any means necessary which is covered legally, I might add. Incidentally, I think that Malcolm X was an incredible man. He will forever be remembered for his original pro-violence reputation philosophy, just as you will be known for your reputation. I am not passing judgment here, but I am stating the facts. In reality, Malcolm X matured and changed his separation views. http://en.wikipedia.org/wiki/Malcolm_X X was a wise, life-experienced, insightful man determined to assist the black community. His journey was one of growth, influence and achievement. You do not have that luxury of taking the time to reflect or ponder in law enforcement. It is often sound bites and liability off the cuff stuff for you. You are part of this big machine known as the wheels of justice. Though there has been a push to validate the justification and legitimacy of criminal justice as a discipline. The overall program concept goals have not changed. The problem once again is that they are mostly supervisors, administrators, and figure heads grabbing these adjunct professor- type Criminal Justice program teaching / instructing positions.

In general, most of this segment of the academic community has done little actual fieldwork, or they are just padding their pockets or résumé instead of focusing on providing you—the student "customer / consumer" with the knowledge, skills or actual requirements you think you need to gain full-time, meaningful employment. These latter law enforcement types may provide you with a war story or two, but do not be fooled—the degree frankly will not serve you well.

How Does Your Background Check Out?

Any background investigation will include character references, neighborhood interviews, school reference checks, and extensive reviews for any and all law violations. This includes traffic violations and all the things you forgot about in your youth or the long ago past. Therefore, the threshold for the aspiring applicant becomes just this simple: Hold yourself from today to that higher standard. If you have no close formal family, religious or structured upbringing or know how, here is some off the cuff crash course stuff that typically eludes many of today's American self-serving "it's all about me" youth:

1. Do not get intoxicated and drive. Drink responsibly and get a ride home if in doubt about your sobriety.
2. Do not get into physical altercations unless saving a damsel in distress, an old lady from a purse snatcher, or obviously saving yourself from a tremendous butt kicking (though running away is better for you the applicant, sad as it is to say).
3. Do not pay for sex.
4. Don't view child pornography. If you are a viewer, you have a problem and definitely should not consider being an officer. This includes trips to Thailand for young child sex encounters.
5. Do not smoke marijuana or make the lame, Loserville excuse that it is natural or should be legalized. I arrested a jackass criminal justice major for carrying the stuff while he was driving in 2010. How stupid. Take a page from Jesus when he states in the Bible : "Give to Caesar what is Caesar's (on the issue of paying taxes)." Luke 20:25. Marijuana *is* illegal– period, unless you have a California prescription for it for your glaucoma. Buy a hemp shirt and drive on!
6. Do not sell drugs – weed, coke, crack, heroin, meth, oxycontin, or any synthetic equivalent, etc. The real reason to not sell drugs is because, in the words of Mr. T.: "Fool." You don't want to deal with those big, badass inmates in prison. Don't shoot it, snort it, smoke it or swallow it because it is also still illegal and it's called possession. Stop going to Hookah lounges!
7. Do not be charged with beating, raping, or threatening a woman. Your name is mud here and you are done. This is a political hot potato, and if you did it, your actions are completely unacceptable. If you are a decent person, then the secret to this one is mostly in the selection process: choose your mate wisely and correct as needed. It would also be in your best interests to disassociate from

drug dealers, a meth-using family member, or a friend who happens to be drug addict. It will spell major trouble for you.

In Case Your Moral Compass Is Broken

A sure fire way to find out if you are cut out for this profession and if you can successfully pass a background is to simply review your own life experience.

Again, a visit to http://www.youtube.com/watch?v=QR465HoCWFQ to take the time to watch Chris Rock's unofficial television show skit is a great lesson. The skit provides that wisdom on "How not to get your ass kicked by the police." Although it is intended as a comic look, it is an absolute litmus test of the real life drama playing out in our communities. Check your past thoroughly before a background investigator does. Gauging your moral compass is the precursor to your measurement of acceptability.

Measurement of Acceptability

My value system was forged years ago when I was a young child. Back then, there were three television channels that went off the air after three o'clock in the morning. I would listen to the "Star Spangled Banner," which instilled pride in my country and made strong references to honor and duty. By contrast, my two teenage sons stayed out all night because their mom let them and because she wanted to be her sons'"friend." Along with the rest of our oblivious society, they watch the regular primetime murder, mayhem, horror and gore way past the old three o'clock in the morning cutoff time and without any sense of honor, duty, or code. Thanks cable television! It is truly a shame. Years of parochial grade school cannot right the wrongs that have become acceptable in our mainstream culture. Female Rap Artist Nonchalant has a great 1995 song to this point "5 o'clock in the morning" http://www.youtube.com/watch?v=WHwHW1O7I8I

Connected but Not Tied

As I mentioned before, I have witnessed death up close and personal several times. Watching those gasps of the last breath or the gurgle of blood in the mouth as they searched my face while I saw the desperate gut wrenching hollow fear was *not* cool.

Music lyrics blare in the car for you, America, and unfortunately, my teens at every trip; en route to anywhere reinforcing the selfish, gruesome and just plain ignorant rants of some of the most wealthy assholes in our societies elite who we often call "music artists." The result is that the subliminal message of anyone else's problems is not my concern. Television keeps most of you and my kids connected but definitely not tied in emotionally. The City of Pittsburgh dropped the ball on 12-12-12 making it Wiz Khalifi day in the burgh; where he announced on Twitter "Get Stoned" and posed with City Council wearing a hat that said "Dope." Yes, financially successful in the rap music industry and young filled with mistakes; but just plain wrong in my eyes. Especially on the five year anniversary of Cpl. J. Pokorny's murder. http://www.youtube.com/watch?v=FDhqHvnLbFl http://www.post-gazette.com/stories/local/neighborhoods-city/ pittburgh-city-council-makes-12-12-12-wiz-khalifa-day-665879/

Growing up with asthma and other severe allergies, I was absolutely tied in emotionally and I honestly suffered tremendously. No whining, but many near death (no exaggeration) experiences have a way of getting you locked on and in tune with what actually matters. I grew to understand empathy and appreciate difficulty with every hospital visit.

Difficulty and Despair

This book is absolutely about you and what you should know. I hope you truly come to understand that the real deal for you is "difficulty and despair," which is the law enforcement mantra, regardless of your job assignments, department, or location. I have grown to appreciate the struggles of my fellow man. It is the ultimate lesson in humility if you are paying attention. Dead children and the commonality of extreme violence make most of us in the profession callous beyond belief, just so we can function and remain effective. Cruelty and venom often spew from the law enforcement officer's mouth because humans adapt to their environment.

Honestly, the working police officer should be held in the highest regard just like the service member in the military; since both must function at high levels from within the belly of the beast. Evil is real. I listened to a revision of a convicted criminals joke about how he could not remove a head with a dull ax on a homicide where they argued over alcohol. In contrast, we are challenged and reprimanded for swearing at criminals? I have often wondered how as a civilized people we can be so violent towards each other with little if any remorse. Alcohol and drugs certainly play a significant role. But, how many times have you seen severely disabled people wearing a huge smile while healthy "no values" clowns in our society are complaining about their petty plight in life?

Mentally Strong

It is going to be hard to manage stress for a twenty-five-year-plus career if you are not mentally and emotionally strong in your values and foundation. Police are unbelievably hard on each other—relentless, in fact. What about you? Can you take it? Who has shaped your value system, or is your moral compass broken already? This job requires people skills, decision-making and serious time management. However it also mandates, *at least in inception*, a very high degree of moral character, integrity and trust. Again, it is a value system not borne out of an innocent life; it honestly comes through life experience with people. Very few people go through this job unscathed. The ones that do are self-servers. You must have a family group, church group or other value-based system to survive, even if it is a system of loosely knit friends. So, how do you qualify and maintain?

Managing Accountability and Productivity

Law enforcement is accountability in its most basic form, whether policing, corrections or juvenile probation. Currently, our culture makes excuses for people. I do not mean to diminish hard times. No one makes it in this world alone. Everyone needs a helping hand from time to time. The lessons of adversity and mistakes shape our future. Having had an incredibly difficult childhood, I have been down just as far as most of the bad guys in the street. I resided in about thirty-one different homes before I turned twenty-one. I was a juvenile dependent ward of the Allegheny County Court at age fourteen. Severe, life threatening allergies and asthma have afflicted me my entire life. I know suffering and pain well and by their first names. But I do not complain or cry poor me. I feel one hundred percent blessed. Believe it!

Law Enforcement Forces Responsibility

Law enforcement forces responsibility. Let that sink in. Find out if your personality is compatible to taking charge and holding people accountable. Bad guys don't always go willingly just because you say they should.

First, you should have faith in something and then a plan for some immediate and long term goals. Second, love your job, your life, your family, your dreams, even your paycheck. It can be whatever wakes you at night or puts you at rest. This is a good indicator and motivator of what you might be designed for. Third, be realistic. Life can become a complicated mess. You can thrive with focus and intestinal fortitude, which is a blend of character, conviction and a heaping helping of tons of hard work.

Perseverance and Patience

Chapter 23 of Dale Carnegie's *How to Stop Worrying and Start Living* carries the heading, "How to Add One Hour a Day to Your Waking Life." It refers to the importance of getting sufficient rest—something you are going to absolutely need to carry out your job. Carnegie cites a convincing study conducted in Pennsylvania to increase steel worker productivity. The study concluded that a physical worker can do more work if he takes more time out for rest. Be prepared to be bombarded with paperwork and requirements that will frustrate disgust and make your head spin. Deal with it, develop perseverance and patience. Wear your groove, gradually. Low morale is not uncommon in police departments. http://www.dalecarnegie.com

Keep in mind upon arriving at, or near, retirement most police officers die of stress related illnesses, i.e., heart attack, stroke, cholesterol, high blood pressure, cancer or alcoholism. The average life expectancy is fifty-seven years. *Decide today to exceed that limitation.*

Definitely a Leader

Again, the key to survival in police work or any job for that matter is applying your substance, reason for existence and life experience lessons with balance. You should never just go with the flow; but work to serve others and do your personal best. As a police officer, you are often that leader who gains tremendous life experience through the thousands of citizen contacts. As I mentioned earlier in this book;

Remember: (We live and function in a society that seems to demand perfection and no mistakes. Yet, it is those that have survived and lived through the emotions of despair, disappointment and failure that know the most). Leaders decide. They set a course, execute a goal or just demand a change. When they drift off course they refocus. Most recently, many amazing people emerged as heroes and leaders in the Boston marathon bombings and the aftermath. Those Leaders included the Emergency workers, Doctors, Nurses, Volunteers, Runners, and the Victims themselves.

Many of Life's leader lessons and champion training can include any of the following:

- Financial hardships;
- The hurdles of fighting or sharing with brothers and sisters siblings;
- Death of a loved one;
- Becoming the victim of a crime – assault, bad relationship, etc.;
- Any tragedy;
- Building a work ethic;
- Team sports, boxing or mixed martial arts; and
- Learning a skill or a trade.

Along with a million other examples that make it is easy to relate to people and their setbacks. The limitations you place on yourself will determine your level of success or achievement. Train yourself to be the best. Foolish officers meet the paperwork requirements for their department and think (or pretend) that they've done good work. Healthy does not always mean productive; in this demanding job, you should have a balance of both.

Values, Reputation, Service—the Service of a Good Pastor

I have been told that it is professional suicide to profess your faith in business because you stand to alienate clients, customers and peers who have different views or denominations or those who are simply non-believers. My response is that any person who would object to a belief system that treats others with love and respect is probably someone I would not want to do business with or endorse, anyway. If by chance, you are offended by my statement of faith, I ask that you reflect on the core values which mean so much and which have helped sustain my career.

Compromise or Conviction?

People with strong political or atheistic views often overlook the main point which is intentions. This is even the same mistake of extremist terrorists. People are never entirely one dimensional. Instead, we are basically the sum total of our experiences and then the reaction to those experiences. The point I am making here is that for law enforcement, we only look at the intentions of a person when assessing culpability. We never ever compromise on a person's intentional criminal acts. Yet, we still treat criminals professionally and with a code of conduct. I could have found plenty enough rage to beat the man who killed a fellow officer—Corporal Joseph Pokorny. Cpl Pokorny was shot and killed following a short pursuit near an exit ramp from I-279 in Carnegie, Pennsylvania. Myself and another guy took that weak-ass coward to jail that night. Every fiber in my body wanted to hurt him to the depths of my soul. http://www.post-gazette. com/stories/local/uncategorized/homicide-trial-of-leslie-mollett-in-the-killing-of-trooper-joseph-pokorny-504145/

Law enforcement professionals should be people of strong moral values and convictions. Do not ever, ever negotiate, or surrender, the just beliefs of right and wrong. Always weigh the totality of the situation or circumstances to assess what is at stake.

Putting the Best Foot Forward.

I have put my best foot forward to carefully consider *your best interests*. I still have friends from the first grade and I have been all over the world! Homicide suspects and felonious men with whom I have had violent encounters look me squarely in the eye, and I return the gaze just as intently. It is communication based on integrity, my honest actions and a good life. I have no reason at all to bow my head. Without a foundation rooted in faith, a hope for a better whatever, and the love of someone or something meaningful, you will be lost and will fail to get past the basic background requirements for employment. As for me and my house; we are filled with mistakes and sometimes without house, we serve the Lord. To be sure, I am a complete and foolish sinner filled with human error and repeated failure.

In basic training, you will learn that you represent something much bigger than yourself, and that includes the concept of you never let anyone disrespect the uniform. The reason is that the criminal or out of control person will do it again the next time. What's more, you have a duty an obligation to serve and make the situation better. Otherwise, your failure to act may have cost another officer or a citizen their life. That means that I never could beat everyone up before the job and I still cannot on the job. Absolutely No Clark Kent to Superman syndrome here. However, if I am dispatched, you should know that I come to handle business and I do not take bullshit from anyone. Regardless of size, disposition or ability. Not because I have a complex or little man Napoleon Syndrome—but instead just because I do in fact represent something much bigger than myself; which is real law and order.

Reflect What You Believe

So when my mistakes and sin do not get free passage from man, and God sees that I continue to mess up, I can say that I really honestly tried my best. It is true that, like Peter, I have denied the Lord without ever hearing a rooster crow. But, I will not deny the Lord when I have had time to reflect, write and review this publication. I have lived and functioned in this society just like you. In the process bombarded with all kinds of perverse lies and sin daily. In policing, I have interviewed awful killers who have dismembered bodies; arrested crazy "actors" who are high out of their mind and covered in sticky blood; and fought with many men in between; none of which has aided my peace of mind. I once had a small dude chained to the floor during arrest growling like a tiger, high from smoking "wet"; which is embalming fluid (a chemical solvent used for dead body preservation). Criminals dip cigarettes and marihuana joints in the fluid and then hallucinate for hours; I was truly afraid of this violent moron.

Just dealing with the daily drunk driver wears you down due to the violence, chases, and overall liability when they fall or get hurt. How tragic it is when people of sound character make these mistakes or poor judgments. Those persons who foolishly celebrate with enough alcohol to be over the legal limit, getting into their car, only to weave down the road and wipe out others lives. I witnessed my coworker investigate the deaths of an entire family gone due to one individual's foolish, split second thoughtless selfish "I deserve this" birthday celebration actions. Such careless behavior is nothing short of a reckless act from someone who simply did not recognize the big responsibility. As police officers, how are we to maintain faith in something and act with professionalism? Understand that drinking and driving has real consequences: http://www.madd.org

Violence, mayhem and predatory persons are just the tip of the iceberg in a society filled with the daily garbage of criminals who constantly commit thefts and marketing fraud. Fighting these criminals is a basic activity in police work. If you have seen internet pornography or listened to offensive music lyrics or even watched recent movies; you know that chivalry and civility has died. The Temptations' old hit song "Treat her like a Lady" should be a mandatory video for children to watch in schools. Check out the 1985 music video on Youtube: http://www.youtube.com/watch?v=PPUsQDm-HQY Plus they have easy to learn dance moves!

Accountability

Confusion is an inevitable norm for the masses. It really becomes essential in this life to determine who to trust and what path to take. I hope you take the path I have carefully laid out *for your profession*. Integrity is based on accountability. Accountability is another way to say, "I am responsible and I can be trusted." Being trusted at its core means you have the religious values of family and a civilized society at heart. I say religious values, because, regardless of your faith, this is where such values originate. I once heard a radio pastor say that men could not walk the street if it were not for the church. He is indeed correct, and he meant that without faith; the powerful (like those in a gang armed with superior weapons) would otherwise dominate the meek. If you are still in doubt, check your history. I specifically refer to the Ten Commandments from the Bible. Unless you are familiar with a conduct reference book that predates the Bible, you should probably (or absolutely!) consider God first before all.

Although there are various translations, I have turned to the NIV (New International Version) translation here below as translated from verses 14-15, in the book of Exodus found in Chapter 20:2–17 and in the book of Deuteronomy, Chapter 5:6–21 (verses 6 thru 21). Review the first five of the commandments on God's instructions to man on your relationship with the Lord.

1. You shall have no other gods before me. (Peace, Eternal Salvation; Foundation. Faith, Structure, Direction, Focus).
2. You shall not make for yourself anything in the form of an idol in heaven above or earth. (No false God's or love of material objects).
3. You shall not misuse the name of the Lord your God. (Do not use the Lord's name in vain; the absolute worst swear word that will not go unpunished).
4. Remember the Sabbath (Sunday) by keeping it holy (Day of rest and obligation).
5. Honor thy Father and Mother so that you may live long in the land the Lord is giving to you. (Respect).

(I recognize that your relationship with the Lord, though my duty as a Christian to profess; is not necessarily our focus in acquiring a law enforcement career. And so we move on).

Law Enforcement Is How to Treat Your Fellow Man.

These next five commandments are your bread and butter for law enforcement which provides at the core of every crime a basic and profound guide on how to treat your fellow man. They are also the exact basis for the Crimes Code sections we enforce - for the most part.

6. You shall not murder. (Every single life has value; which is why there is no statute of limitations for murder).
7. You shall not commit adultery (cheating, domestic violence, protection from abuse orders, child pornography, prostitution, bigamy, incest, rape, etc.).
8. You shall not steal. (Theft, stealing gas, cigarettes, Forgery of credit cards, etc.).
9. You shall not give false testimony against your neighbor (Do not lie which includes perjury, false reports to police, unsworn falsifications, etc.).
10. You shall not covet your neighbor's house, wife, or anything that belongs to your neighbor (jealousy, Barratry, envy).

What Is Your Level of Suitability?

So one last example: The moral foundation of my teenage and young adult years was built on good family, Christian values with a Catholic grade school education. I ask you to reflect on identifying your personal moral foundation. If you have ever eaten at the fast food restaurant, Chick-fil-A, you will notice that they are closed on Sunday. This is because it is the Lord's Day—the Sabbath—and considered a day of rest. If you do ever eat there, take the time to grab a business card and look on the back. Here you will find the words, "To glorify God by being a faithful steward of all that is entrusted to us. To have a positive influence on all that come in contact with Chick-fil-A". Founder S. Truett Cathy said in his book, *How Did You Do It, Truett? : A Recipe for Success:* "Our decision to close on Sunday was our way of honoring God and of directing our attention to things that mattered more than our business." I have also made reference to this company because they have great milkshakes! (just kidding-but the milkshakes are pretty awesome!).

When I wrote these statements it was prior to July 31st of 2012. Now, the Truett family is in the news as a large political contributor and a force that opposes same sex marriage. What you should recognize is the power of clarifying your belief system and being committed. So again, what is your base belief system? Pondering this might put to the test those factors deeply situated in your mind that ultimately provide your level of suitability for this profession. In my case it is strong Christian faith. Maybe for you it is something different. Get to know yourself, what you believe and especially the "Why." It is essential since you will be tempted, challenged and at times filled with rage, doubt and despair during the course of carrying out your law enforcement duties.

As someone working to educate you, consider me your informed confidant who is assisting the prospective, yet humble, willing applicant—you. When I attended police basic training, my platoon leader was a corporal in the firearms unit. He always appeared angry. Yelling seemed his favorite pastime each time he stood in front of the class. Usually, that included advising any of us who felt "occupationally misplaced" that we should get out right now. He said it so much that I honestly had to consider whether I was the one he constantly sought to remove. However, since I was over 200 miles from home and I had hitched a ride with a friend of a friend to get there, it occurred to me he must be wrong, and so I decided that his yelling was just noisy rhetoric. It sure is a good thing, too. My "Why" is very powerful, and I have truly served well, remaining productive in policing despite years of stress caused by many things; including those curious piles of meaningless paperwork.

Apply Your Life Experience.

My father passed away from lymphoma cancer; he was hospitalized with no known illnesses initially; but died on his third day in the hospital. At that time my mother already had tremendous financial problems, which were then compounded. It took me ten years to put a headstone on my father's grave. He died with no insurance, retirement, or pension. After his death, I experienced a great deal of unsupervised time, which I "skillfully" used for fooling myself; including pledging my loyalty to the wrong people. Fortunately, I was able to survive through God's grace - delivered with the blessings of a tremendous amount of caring, considerate people around me. Those persons included family, friends, counselors, teachers, neighbors and even strangers. Getting back to values, goals and knowing your "Why" can help avoid the confusion that almost cost me my future. Those goal clarification points might very well help you avoid becoming compromised. Some of my friends made the wrong choices and died of drug addictions. Others committed house burglaries or were violent attackers and lifelong bar room brawlers. A few were murdered in the street like animals. Many became good guys like me and more than a few became excellent police officers. With misdirected loyalties to my friends in the street, I could have easily failed at a police career. Somehow, I managed to maintain the core values which derived from my overall "love your neighbor" ideology. I now know that the many principles like those found in the Ten Commandments allowed me to see a bigger picture. Otherwise, I probably would have remained completely lost and headed down the wrong path.

Street Law

The Old Testament of the Bible lays a very strong foundation of law and has within its historical roots numerous 'eye for an eye' principles subsequently played out by man. This is exactly how street law functions. Street law is what law enforcement basically fights against in a civilized society. Many guys in the street and many more on the prison cell block; will tell you that the person who was stabbed, shot, beat up, murdered or otherwise victimized - deserved it. On one Aggravated Assault case I investigated;

a man who was stabbed in the prison yard suffered a punctured lung. He told me in an interview during the investigation that the eyewitness guard was mistaken. "That is my boy," the victim told me, describing the attacker. The victim walked with a cane and had a severe limp as a result of the stabbing. He was violently stabbed sixteen times with a shank that resembled an ice pick. The interview was a strangely funny conversation; though in truth it was tragically sad. I joked with him, saying, "Well, your boy cut you deep," trying both to get a reaction from him and lure him into making an angry statement. In accordance with street language and this street law; he said next to nothing. Six months, six years—whatever the time and opportunity—one day the stabber would be repaid his debt in street justice and the process would continue. A very depressing and violent way to exist in our culture. Many things are not verbalized but they are stated just the same. Usually, that means the victim snitched, ran their mouth, had a debt of his own, did something to someone else like tell the truth, cooperate with the police, had a drug habit in excess, or otherwise violated street code.

The laws outside the prison walls and off the streets are greater and more righteous, holding life in the highest regard. Street justice is man's basic, animalistic human behavior in contrast to the codes of civilized society. Unfortunately, after you have been on the job, street law consumes you because everyone must adapt to their environment. No one is exempt from the rules on the street. The incident in the news of Marines urinating on the dead Taliban fighters, or the Canadian hockey announcer vocalizing his ideals of torture for terrorists reflect how easily humanity can slip into the mindset of the street. I am no different. Without the values I am urging you to adopt, it is highly unlikely that you will ever get the job and keep it. I urge you to read slowly and weigh the words of *The Lord's Prayer*:

Our Father, who art in Heaven, Hallowed be Thy name.
Thy Kingdom come, Thy will be done, on earth as it is in Heaven.
Give us this day, our daily bread and forgive us our trespasses
As we forgive those who trespass against us.

Lead us not into temptation but deliver us from evil.
(For thine is the Kingdom, the Power and the Glory forever). Amen.

Please do not try to overanalyze me for espousing the Christian principles that I have worked hard to live by. I have legitimately attempted to help you. I recognize some of you will try to find fault and punch tons of holes in my arguments. I also know that I laid it on you extremely thick with the subject of faith here at the end. As a Christian it is my job to witness to you. Consider yourself witnessed, too. Go ahead and judge or dismiss; my truth is the truth, and it speaks too loudly and convincingly to be ignored. The reputation you represent in your background investigation—regardless of your faith—boils down to the same truths. What do your enemies— the guy you fought in high school or the bitter ex-girlfriend—say about you?

What most self-help experts and motivational speakers know is that *life is lived from the inside out.* Essentially, it means that the values you possess and allow to permeate your heart based on the incidents you have experienced in your life, are the ones that have etched their way into your soul and mind; these become you. If you actually possess good values and have been able to avoid most of the liability pitfalls of youth and our society overall; then you are eligible for a law enforcement career. A clean criminal background, a good credit score without foreclosures, repossessions, and an excessive number of charge-offs are the basic requirements to assist you in obtaining this professional liability based career. Please, always remember that these are *basic eligibility requirements* and they do not speak to the physical, mental, and life experience or people experience requirements that you also need to possess.

Clean up your credit yourself or with a reputable company. Prepare a list of quality references and know what they potentially can and will say about you. Know, document, and review your life history. This definitely includes any and all contacts with the police, from speeding violations to juvenile pranks.

Take the time to review your belief system on paper if practical. Then measure it against the knowledge provided in this book. An applicant should have their mind right for accountability, teamwork and a paramilitary style organizational career. In short, learn to listen, be obedient and capable of following orders. *Obedience is a character strength, not a weakness, as this society would have you believe.*

Organize your life for peak performance and get in legitimate physical shape. Do not show up for the background, polygraph, physical assessment or Basic Training as an out-of-shape toad (nice way of calling you a bum). Invest in yourself.

The Lord Jesus Christ is my personal savior. And so I know and acknowledge daily that as soon as I wake up mistakes are made. I am a foolish human sinner incapable of perfection and true total understanding. It is my sincere wish that you enjoy peace, good health and success in all your endeavors. Life is a great gift. Enjoy it. Truly live it. And serve through your actions and the use of your talents.

Key point of this Chapter: *Identify your ideal values, core purpose and faith for maximum achievement.*

"The Final Inspection"

The policeman stood and faced his God,
Which must always come to pass.
He hoped his shoes were shining.
Just as brightly as his brass.

Step forward now, policeman.
How shall I deal with you?
Have you always turned the other cheek?
To My church have you been true?"

The policeman squared his shoulders and said,
"No, Lord, I guess I ain't,
Because those of us who carry badges
Can't always be a saint.

I've had to work most Sundays,
And at times my talk was rough,
And sometimes I've been violent,
Because the streets are awfully tough.

But I never took a penny,
That wasn't mine to keep.
Though I worked a lot of overtime
When the bills got just too steep.

And I never passed a cry for help,
Though at times I shook with fear.
And sometimes, God forgive me,
I've wept unmanly tears.

I know I don't deserve a place
Among the people here.
They never wanted me around
Except to calm their fear.

If you've a place for me here,
Lord, It needn't be so grand.
I never expected or had too much,
But if you don't...I'll understand.

There was silence all around the throne
Where the saints had often trod.
As the policeman waited quietly,
For the judgment of his God.

Step forward now, policeman,
You've borne your burdens well.
Come walk a beat on Heaven's streets,
You've done your time in Hell."

(Author Unknown)

Commit this humbling poem to memory. It speaks directly to the hardships you will endure.

AFTERWORD

Of making many books there is no end, and much study wearies the body. Now all has been heard; here is the conclusion of the matter:

"Fear God and keep his commandments; for this is the whole duty of man. For God will bring every deed into judgment, including every hidden thing, whether it is good or evil." Ecclesiastes 12:12-14 NIV translation.

ACKNOWLEDGEMENTS

My sincere heartfelt thanks to my family; they are incredibly kind, loving, generous people. Additionally, to the many tremendous friends and associates who have helped me to become the man I am today. I never would have been able to complete this project without Carla's original typing and never ending support. Even to those who would call me an enemy, I must say thank you! How blessed I have become. Literally born and raised in the Valley of Steel—the Mon Valley of the Greater Pittsburgh metropolitan area, which bears the name for all of the steel mills that employed generations in the area; including my own family. I am filled with the pride of cherishing a solid work ethic and good family values. I worked extremely hard to earn everything; some of which I subsequently lost! In the process, like all who find success on the path of life lessons; I received educational failures; exposure to despair; turmoil and those trials which can cause men to crumble. Reducing me at times to a mere shell of what I could have been. Adversity does build character and its defeats do provide any person the tools to succeed; if determined enough to keep going. Without question, I tempted fate by getting close to the fire. I almost got burned (permanently failing); because I chose the wrong path more than a few times. This is a reference to poor decision making or hanging out in my youth with friends who chose a criminal lifestyle. Out of humility, and in all honesty, I would not have made it were it not for the grace and mercy of God, who uses all things for his glory and overall good.

———————

This book was written in the honor of *all* the men and women who wear the uniform, work hard and serve proudly. These servants are not readily identifiable for their good deeds because many talk rough and act aggressively. Yet, they often have hearts of gold buried like hidden treasure, and their actions reflect the true intentions of the strong character within.

My sincere gratitude goes out to each of the troopers and officers with whom I have had the privilege to work. The list is far too extensive to name everyone here; and I am very reluctant to name any active members, anyway. But for those of us who have served together, please know that the stories and incidents we have shared are *forever etched in my soul*. I acknowledge you proudly, and share tremendous respect for each of you- *be safe*. Also in loving memory, and out of that respect, I must honor the following fellow Troopers: Their ultimate sacrifice has left a profound void in their respective families; and I will *never* forget to memorialize them:

- Trooper Tod Kelly who was run over on State Route 79;
- Trooper Joe Sepp who was shot in the head in Ebensburg, PA;
- Trooper Matt Bond whose head was crushed when a truck tractor struck his cruiser in the Erie, PA area; and
- Corporal Joseph Pokorny who was murdered execution style on the Pittsburgh parkway in Carnegie, PA.

There are unfortunately so many more who have died and deserve recognition; but I personally served with each of these men and knew them as honorable. It remains because of them and those many unnamed who are stressed or have been victimized that I choose to never give up on working to make a difference. I owe a debt I can never repay to these men and their families. I recognize not only all of those who made the ultimate sacrifice, but also the members and the civilian employees with us who have suffered so many stressful personal tragedies. As a law enforcement culture, we have the potential to push people into alcoholism and sleepless stressful nights while the Internal Affairs system and the liability based criminal advocates closely review, monitor and Monday morning quarterback our split second actions. At one time, this profession was a family and regarded as a brotherhood. Now we have largely evolved into just being incredibly tough on each other. I have chosen to acknowledge some of these men because yesterday's tragedies are frequently forgotten. The physical and emotional scars cause some to pay the terribly high price of self-destruction. Honestly there are too many countless Officers, Troopers and friends who deserve special credit for inspiring me to write this book. Two of them I will mention here and include: Trooper Dean Kerklo who I can never acknowledge too much. First for his warrior mindset while in the face of insurmountable adversity; with a bullet in his spine and an incredible amount of emotional scars that he chooses to use for good to help others. Reference this 2000 IACP Award winner here: http://www.post-gazette.com/stories/local/neighborhoods-east/nearly-killed-on-the-job-trooper-to-honor-fallen-officers-in-bike-tour-241446/ . Second: Retired Lieutenant Clifford Jobe for his extensive professional and life experience, which he utilized to serve and inspire thousands of officers as an instructor and expert. www.cliffjobe.com .

SOURCES

Most of the information contained in this book is based on the extensive, professional experience of the author, including:

- Investigations, interviews, prosecutions, personal assaults, reports, court room testimony, search warrants, criminal complaints and other related documents from an over eighteen year career employment as a busy State trooper.
- Personal experience as a Pennsylvania Department of Corrections Officer at the State Correctional Institution at Graterford, Pennsylvania, then the fourth largest prison in the U.S. at that time, including the probationary employment program which mandated working every single post at that institution.
- Personal experience as a United States Army Reserve member who served from January 1990 until March 2001 with an Honorable Discharge From Service and included a 1999 deployment to Bosnia to backfill active duty members' deployment to Kosovo; with previous further deployment service in Japan, Germany, France and all over the United States.
- Personal experience as a professional speaker and a police trainer / instructor, including over five years of experience as a full time academy instructor teaching various components of basic training and ongoing advanced training for veteran law enforcement.

WORKS CITED

Bolles, Richard Nelson. *What Color is Your Parachute?* Berkeley: Ten Speed Press, 2009.

Carnegie, Dale. *How to Stop Worrying and Start Living.* New York: Pocket Books, 1990.

Cathy, S.Truett. *How Did You Do It, Truett? :A Recipe for Success.* Aurora, ON: Looking Glass Press, 2007.

Graham v. Connor, 490 U.S. 386 (1989).

Harr, J. Scott and Hess, Karen M. *Careers in Criminal Justice and Related Fields.* 6th Ed. Wadsworth 2010.

Hill, Napolean. *Think and Grow Rich.* New York: J.P.Tarcher, 1937.

Hill, Napolean. *The Laws of Success.* New York: Penguin Books, 1929.

Howe. MSG Paul R. *Leadership and Training for the Fight.* 2006 AuthorHouse.

Koletar, Joseph W. *The FBI Career Guide.* AMACOM 2006.

Lambert, Stephen and Regan, Debra. *Great Jobs for Criminal Justice Majors.* The McGraw-Hill Companies. 2007.

Morgan, Marilyn. *Careers in Criminolgy.* Lowell House 2000.

Murdock, Mike. *The Uncommon Leader.* The Wisdom Center. 2006.

Pittsburgh Post-Gazette. *"The Costly College Scam,"* Jack Kelly. December 26, 2010 Again July 3, 2012.

Pittsburgh Post-Gazette *"Blast from the past:* Pagans vs Angels" Torsten Ove. March 8, 2002.

Remsberg, Charles. *Tactics for Criminal Patrol, Vehicle Stops, Drug Discovery, and Officer Survival.* San Fransisco: Calibre Press, 1978,1995.

Stephens, W. Richard. *Careers in Criminal Justice. 2nd Edition.* 2002 Person Education Company.

Sherwood Pictures Ministry. *Courageous* Movie. 2011.

Tennessee v. Garner, 471 U.S. 1 (1985.)

Toma, David, and Michael Brett. *Toma: The Compassionate Cop.* New York: Putnam, 1973. *topics.nytimes.com/top/reference/timestopics/.../p/petit.../index.html: Story of Dr. William Petit.*

Tracy, Brian. *Goals.* Berrett-Koehler Publishers. 2003.

Tracy, Brian. *No Excuses. The Power of Self-Discipline.* Vanguard Press. 2010.

U.S. Department of Justice. Community Oriented Policing Services *Vets to Cops* pamphlet e051217473 June 2012. www.cops.usdoj.gov

U.S. Department of Justice Community Oriented Policing Services *Innovations in Police Recruitment and Hiring. Hiring in the Spirit of Service.* DVD. And *Police Recruitment and Retention for the New Millennium.* ISBN: 978-1-935676-28-7 e101027321; November 2010.

U.S. Department of Labor and Statistics. *Protective Services Occupations.* 2010.

www.baltimorepolice.org

www.chp.ca.gov

www.criminaljusticeonlineblog.com

www.crimiinaljusticeusa.com

www.fbi.gov

www.fbijobs.gov

www.ITT-Tech.edu

www.sofmag.com : Story of Roy P. Benavidez. Tango, Mike, Mike.

www.nola.gov

www.nytrooper.com

www.odmp.org

www.officer.com; "Morale in Law Enforcement" by Michael Wasilewski and Althea Olson.

www.policepoems.com/FinalInspection.htm

www.values.com

www.wisegeek.com\how-do-I-become-a-Police-Officer

http://www.youtube.com/watch?v=50RFJfUzNsY Sal Giunta Story
http://www.youtube.com/watch?v=P2plo4FOgIU Chris Rock *"How not to get your ass kicked by the Police"* originally from CR TV show.
http://www.youtube.com/watch?v=PPUsQDm-HQY Temptations ("Treat Her Like a Lady").
Scripture taken from the HOLY BIBLE, NEW INTERNATIONAL VERSION. Copyright 1973, 1978, 1984, by the International Bible Society. Used by permission of International Bible Society.

Jimmy MONK is the Professional Speaker / Trainer / Humorist who delivers "The Resiliency Application." This is a Keynote, Workshop, & Breakout session designed to use your setbacks & failures; as a strength. As the oldest of six and the father of two – Jimmy *truly* understands and shares the importance of relationship assets.

Bringing the valuable training lessons and real life experience as a former Corrections Officer, an Honorably Discharged U.S. Army Reserve Sergeant; and a current over eighteen year veteran Trooper; MONK knows the art of decision making. Programs are provided with moral character, a pure focus on service, with enough "clean" Humor to entertain any audience. These are always offered in a spirit of sincerity to save you time, money and energy. Jimmy is available for Criminal Justice presentations based on this book or programs tailored to your organization's individual needs. www. jimmymonk.com